2016 Olympic Venue - Rio de Janeiro

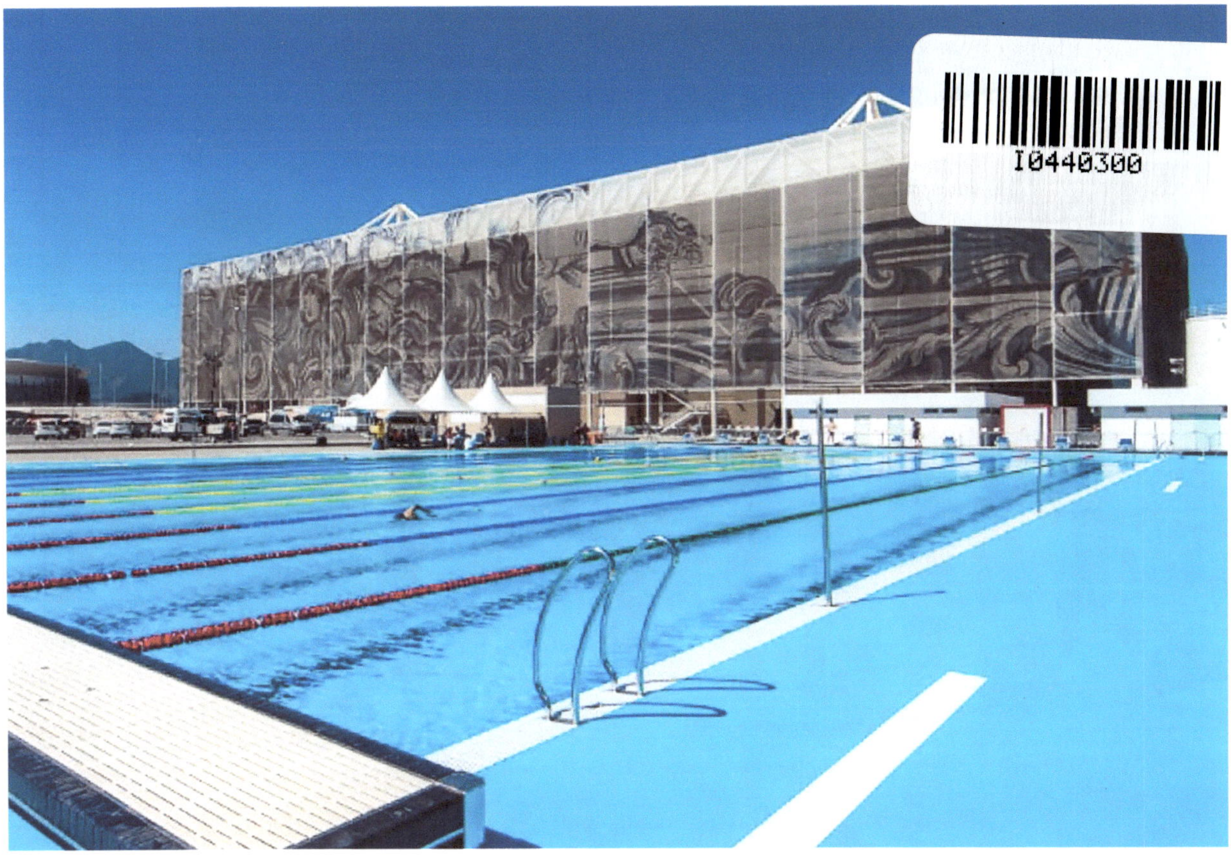

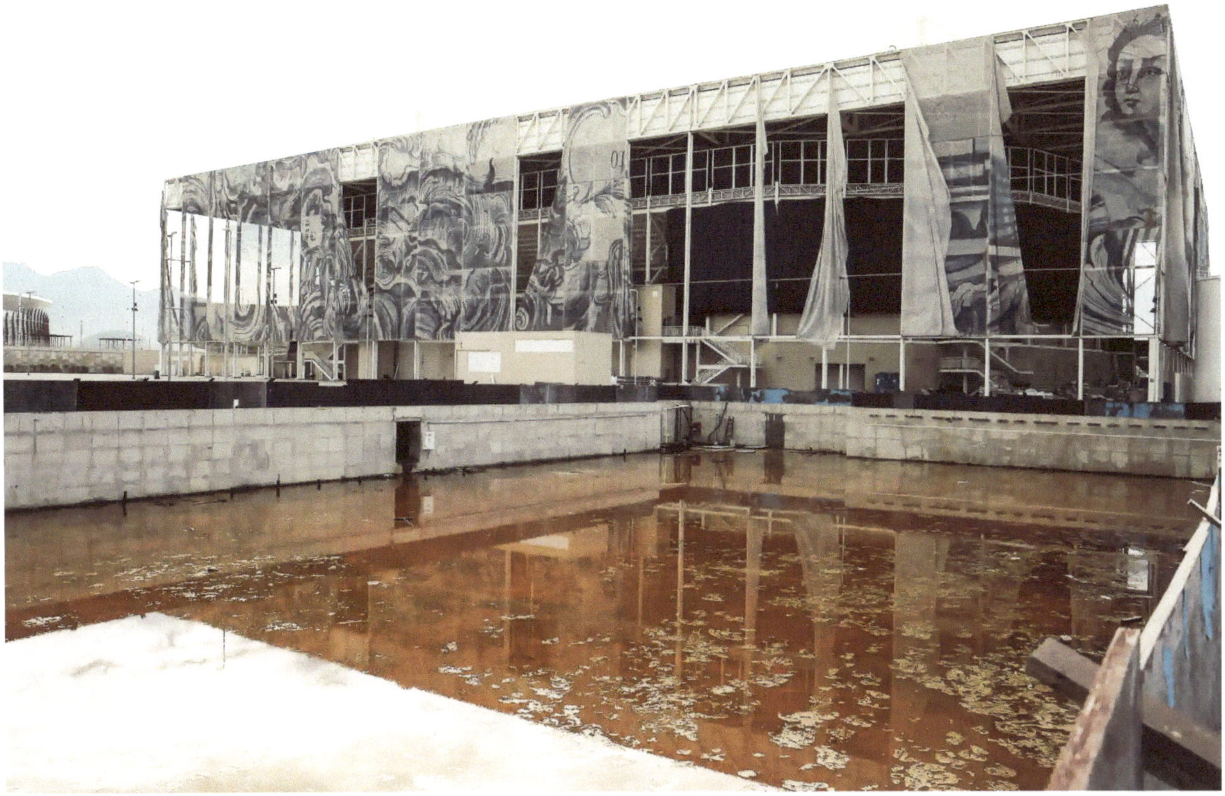

Bank of Commonwealth - Detroit, MI

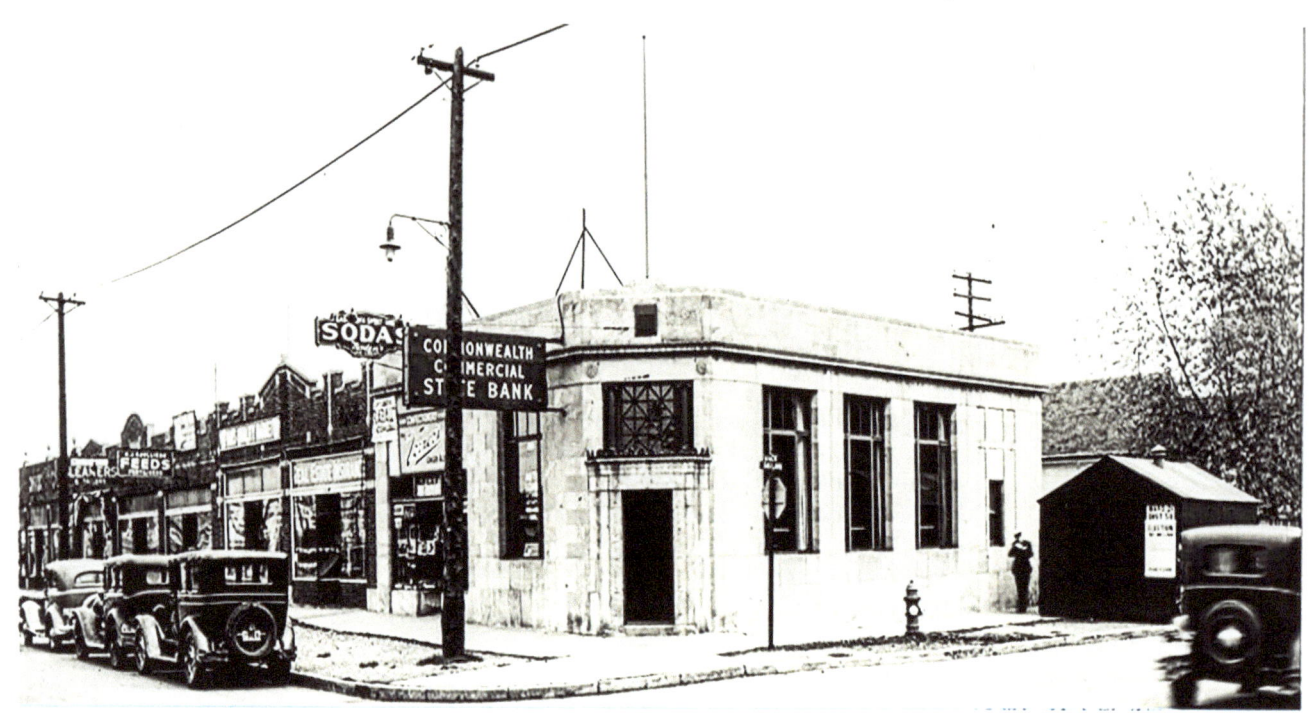

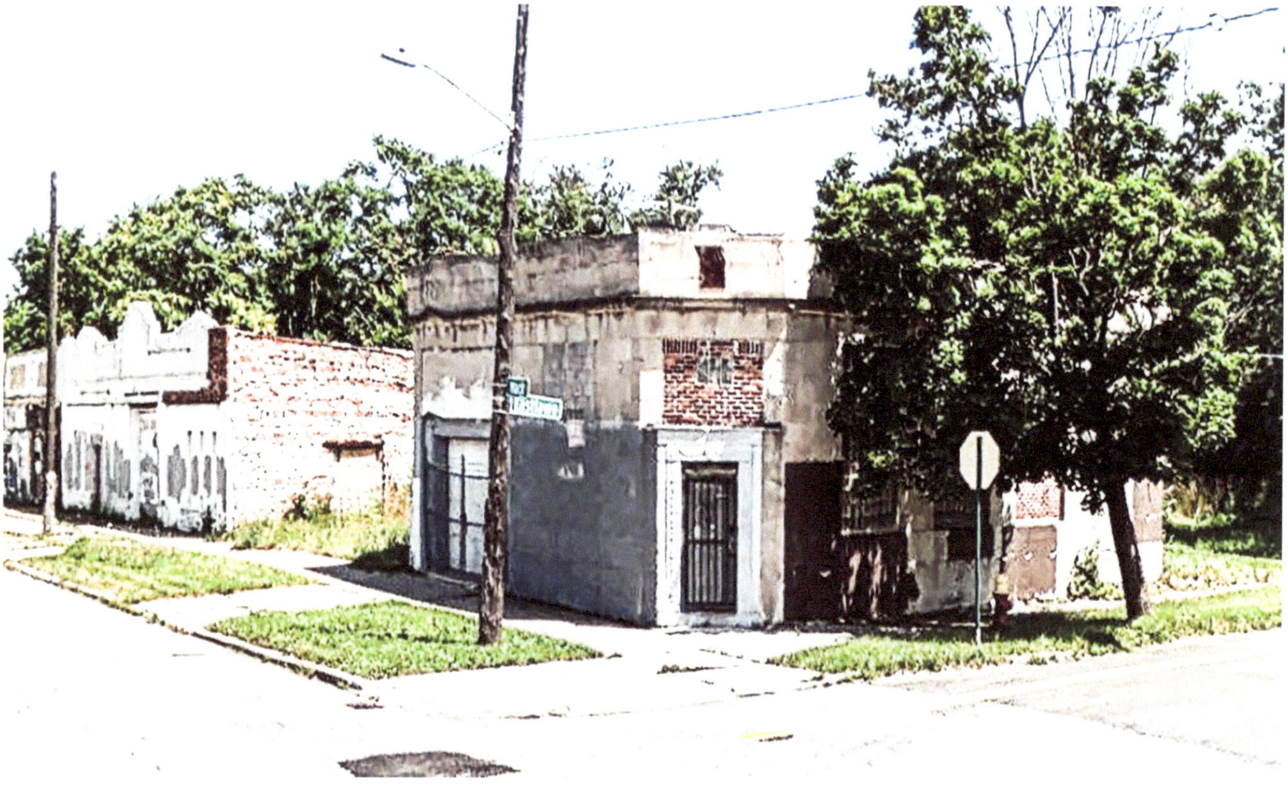

Bowling Homowack Hotel - NY

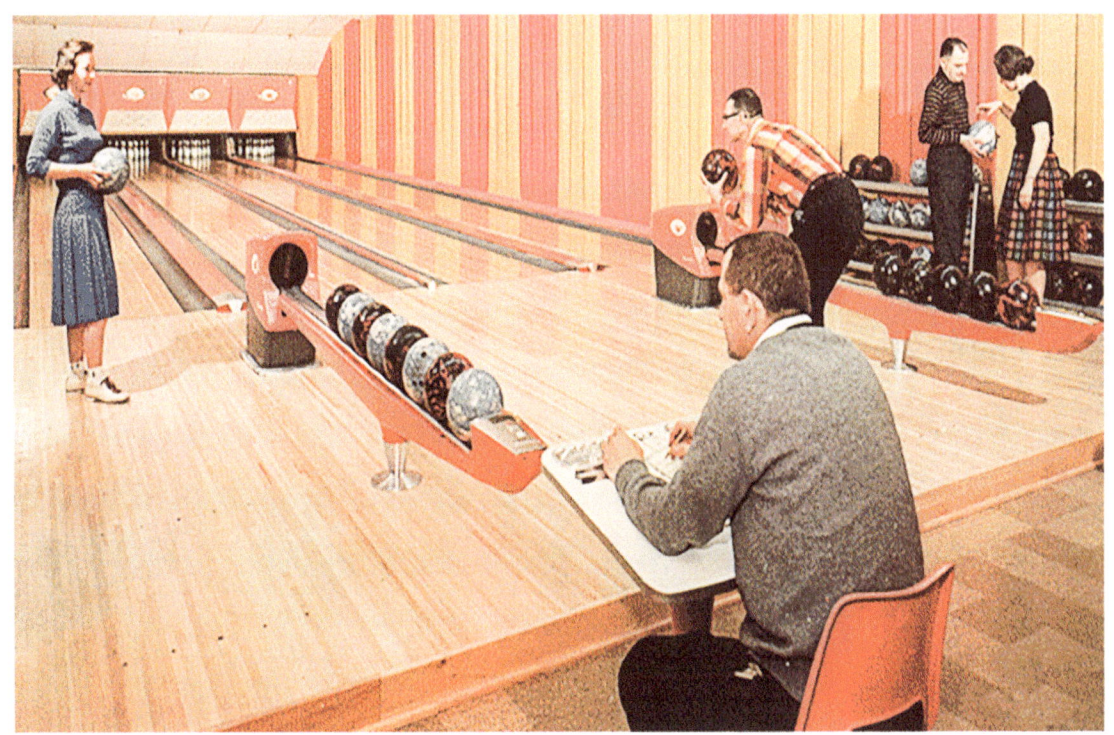

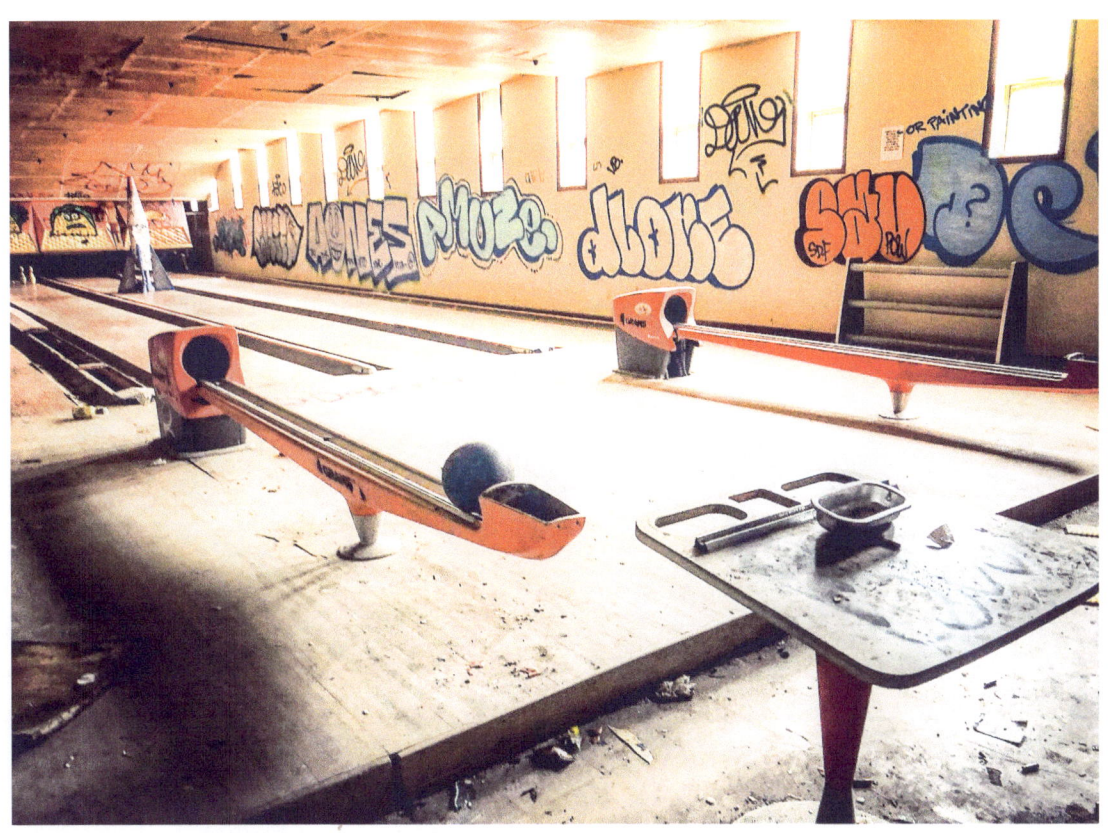

Barefoot Boy of Baker Brook Restaurant in Bethlehem, NH

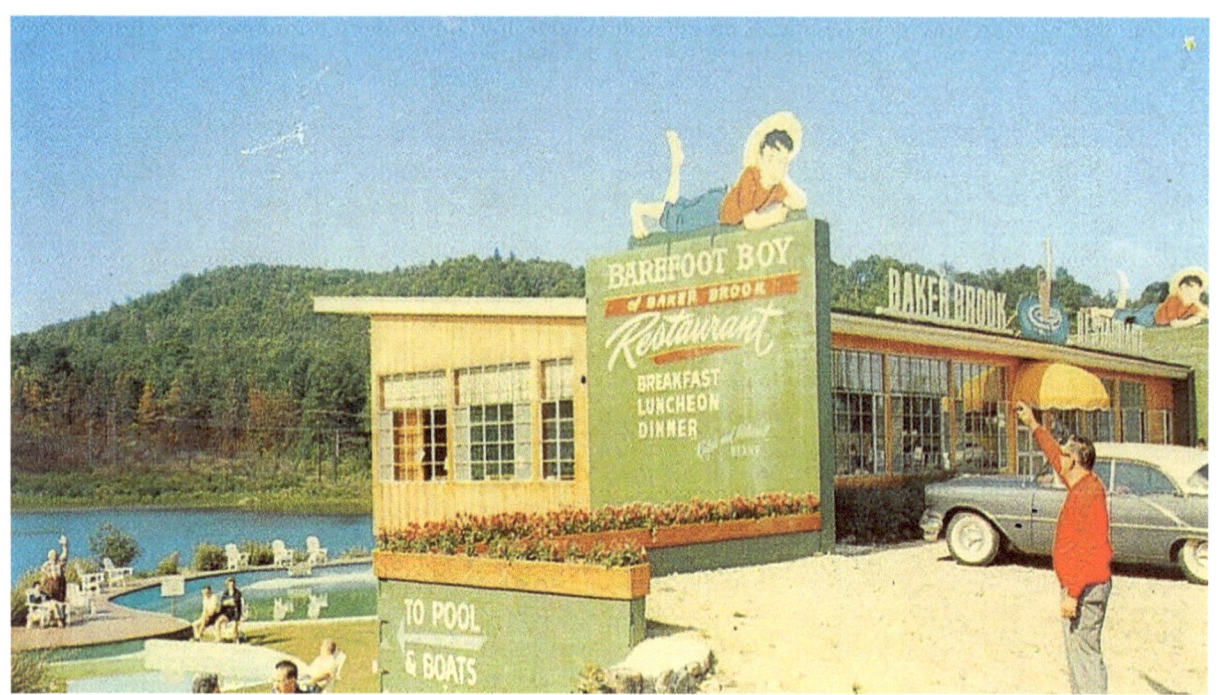

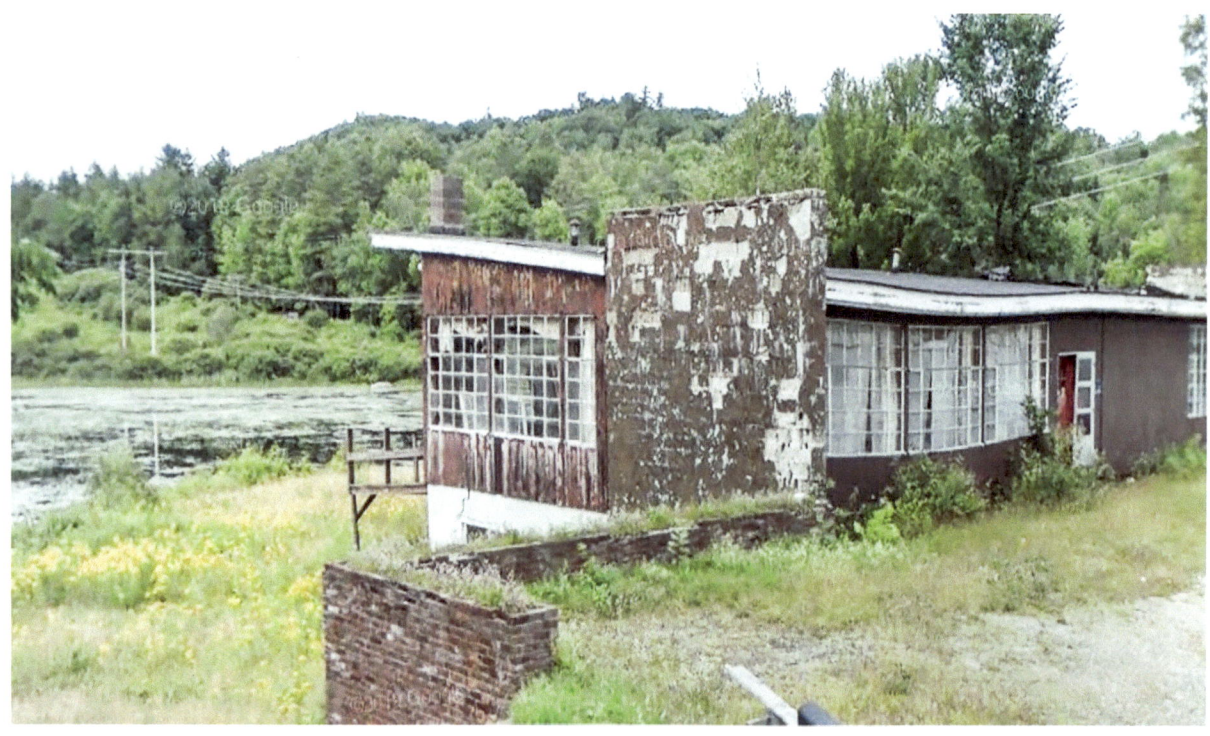

Bennett College - Millbrook, NY

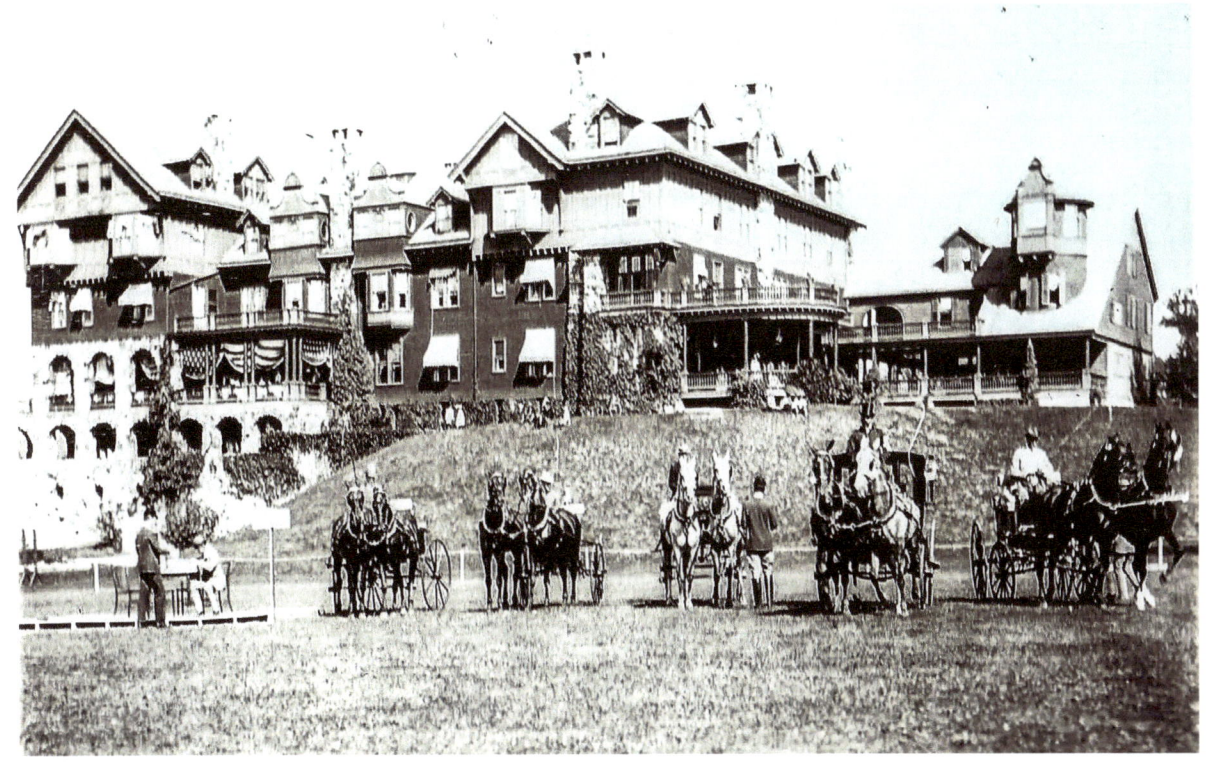

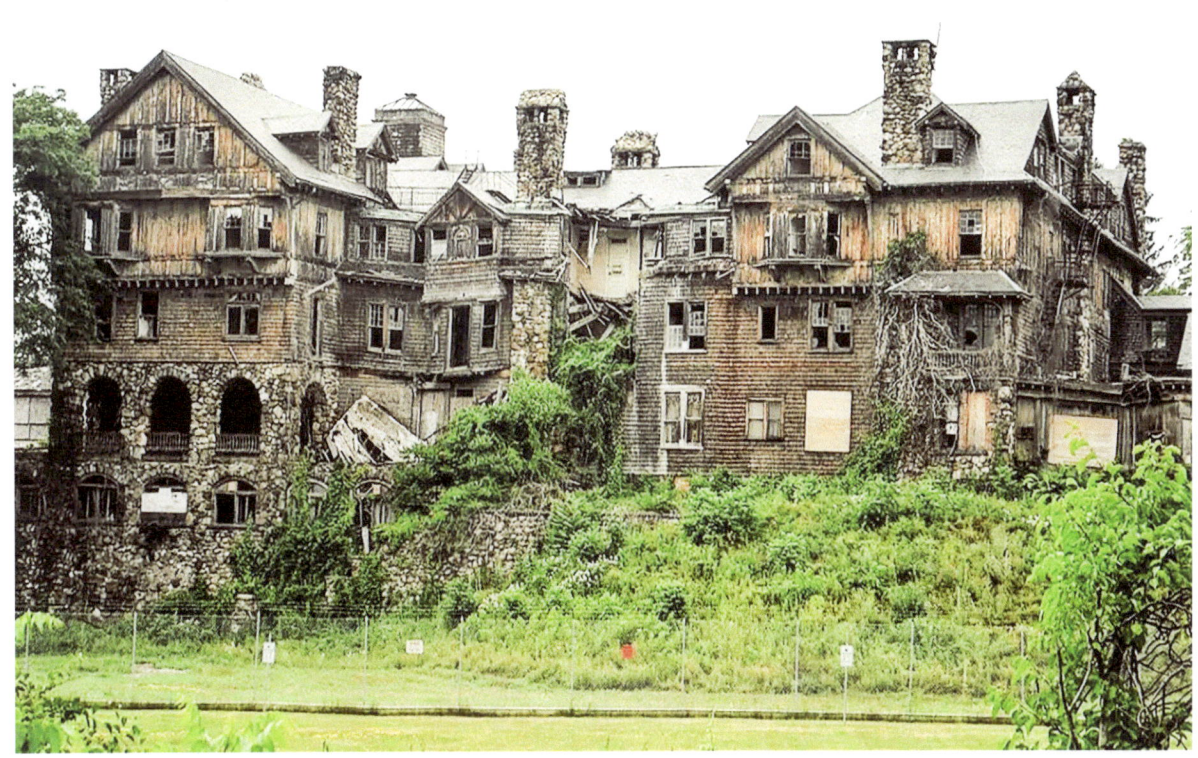

Bluewater Motel - Bluewater New Mexico

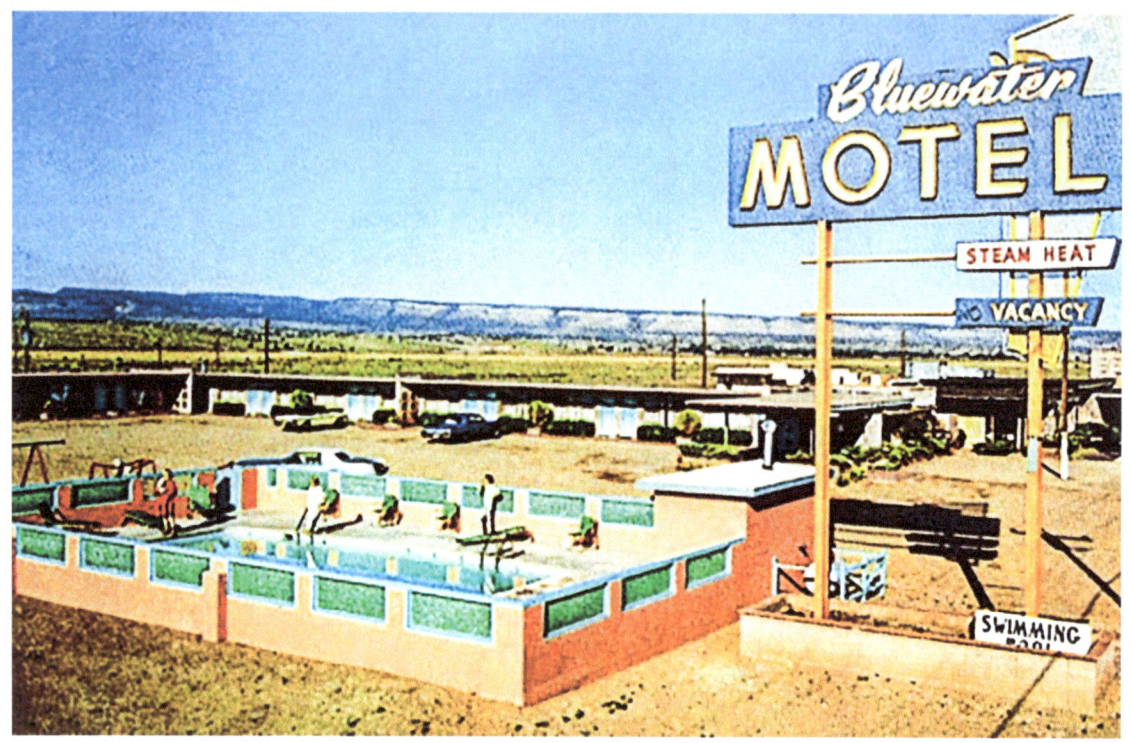

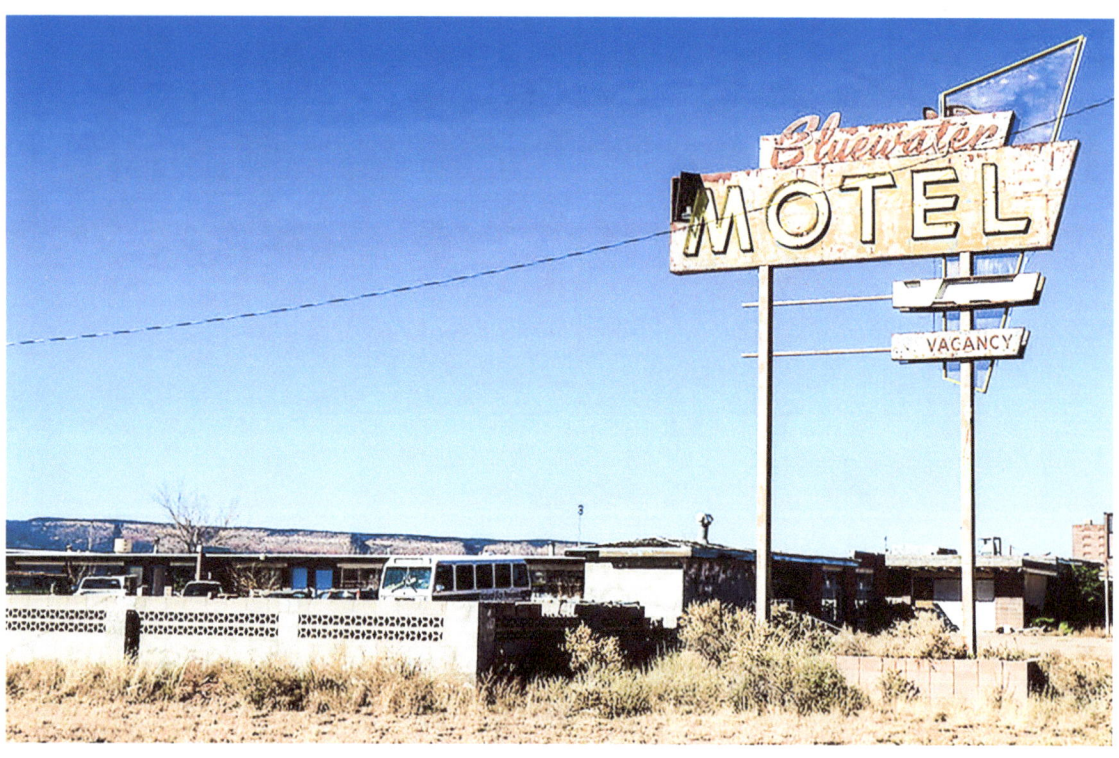

Breakers Water Park - Marana, AZ

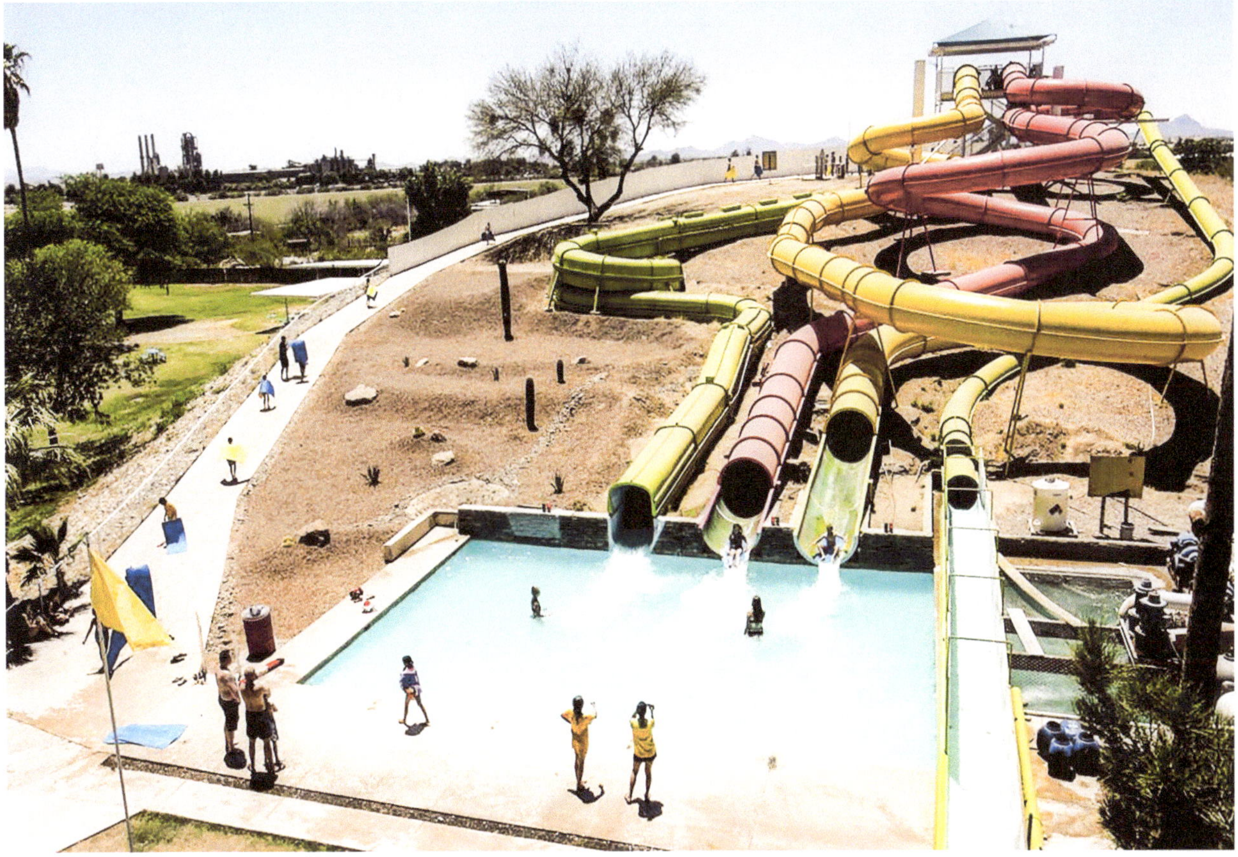

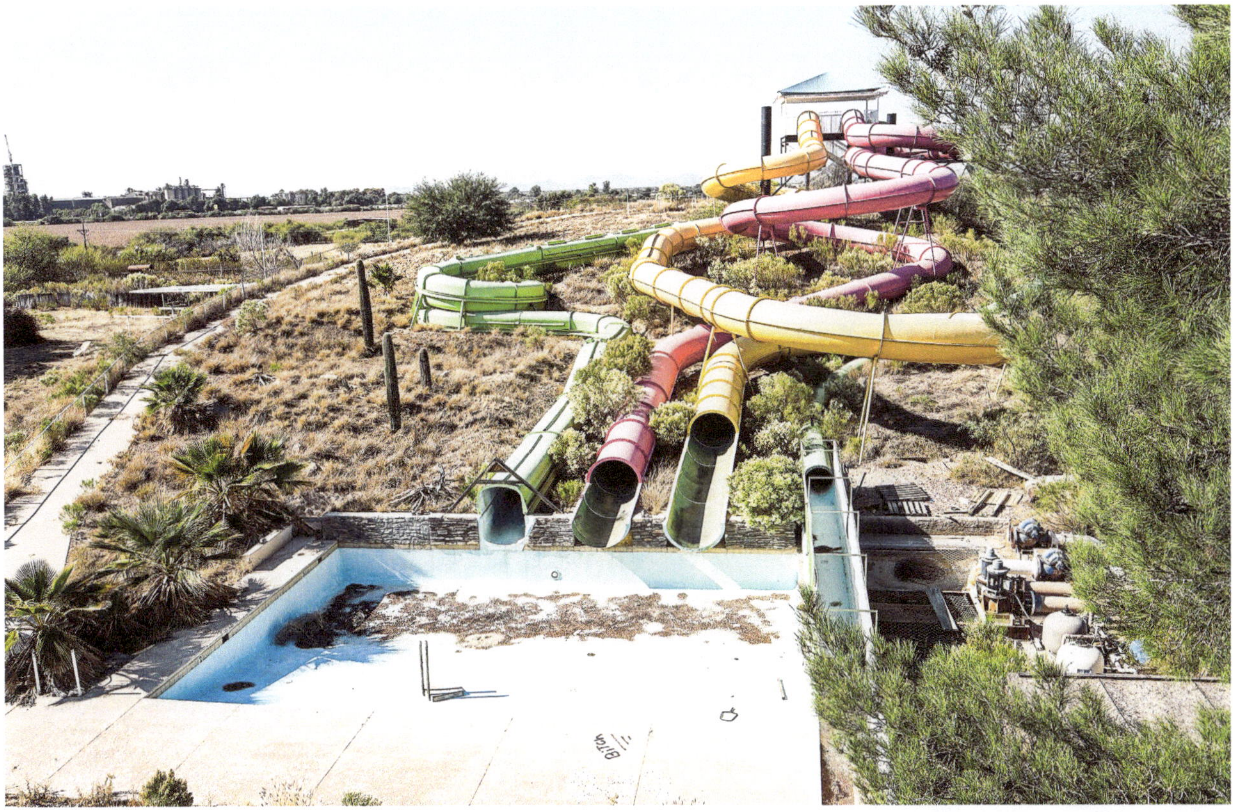

Penn Aire Motel - Breezewood, PA

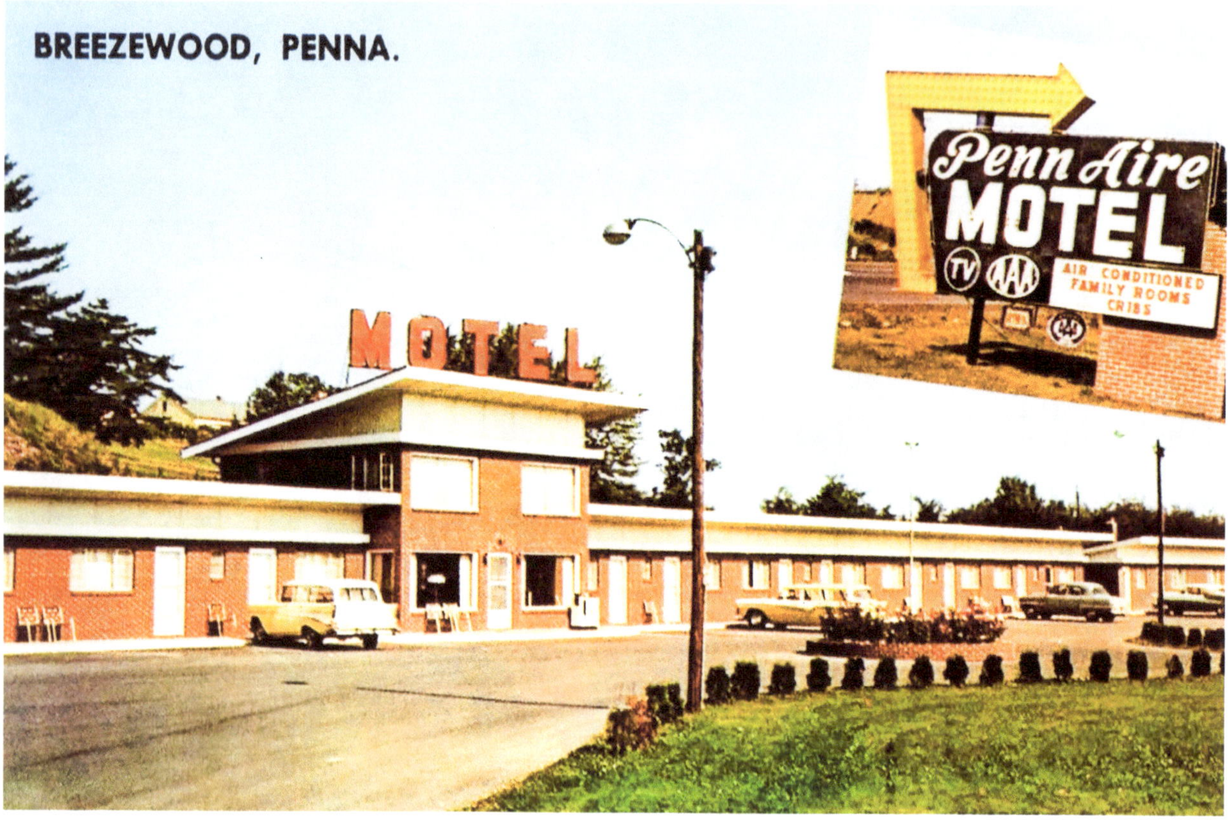

BREEZEWOOD, PENNA.

Penn Aire
MOTEL
TV AAA AIR CONDITIONED
FAMILY ROOMS
CRIBS

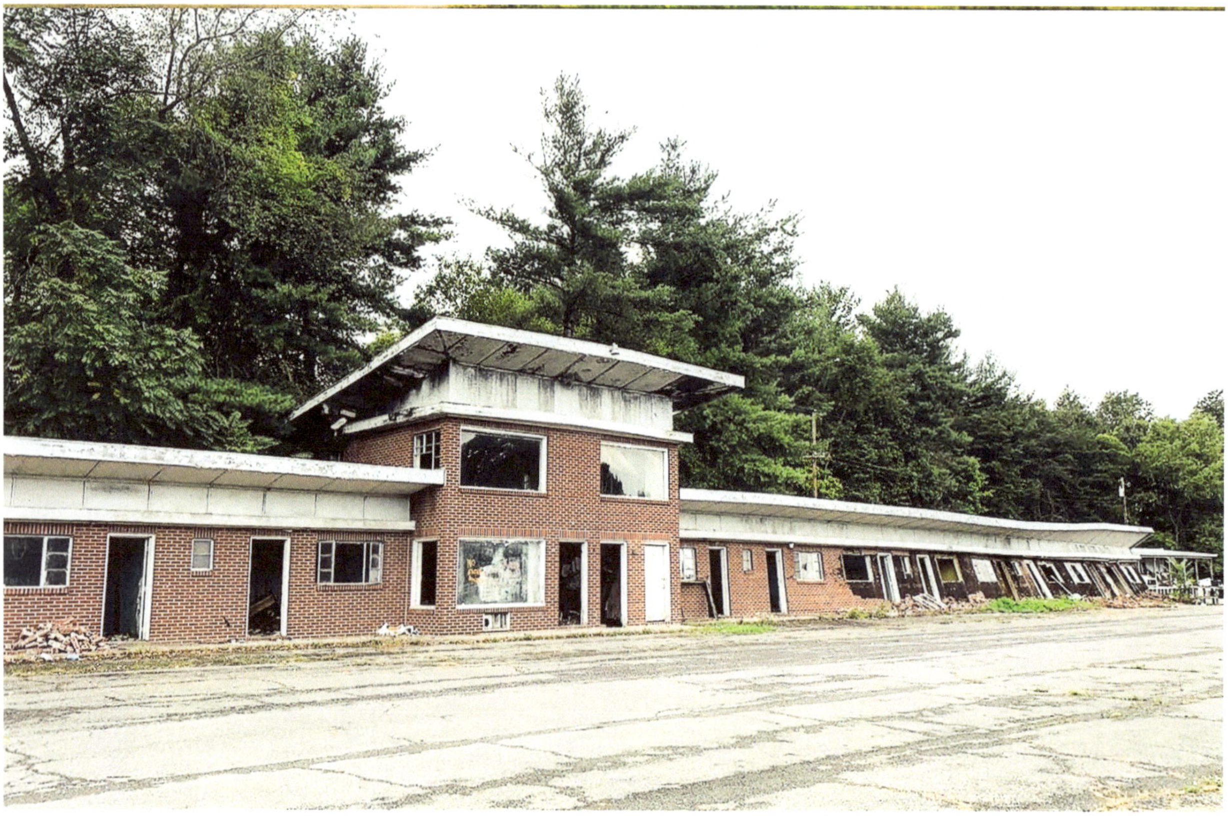

MOTEL

Days Inn - Danville, PA

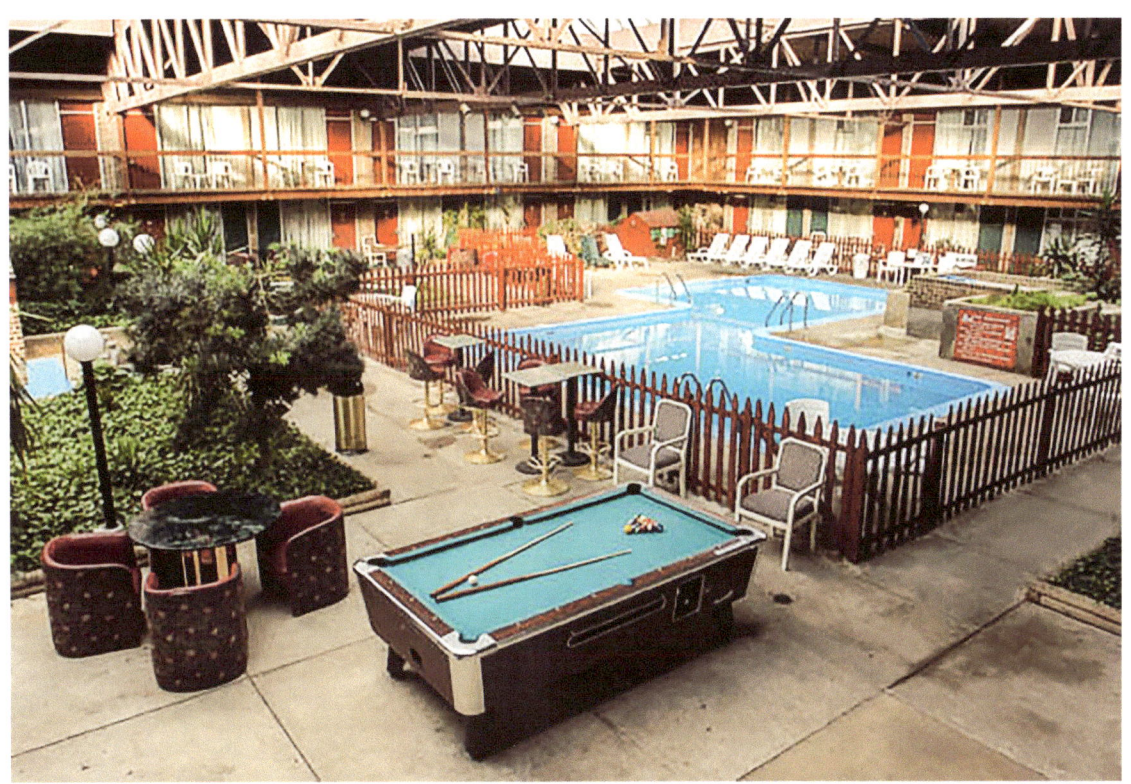

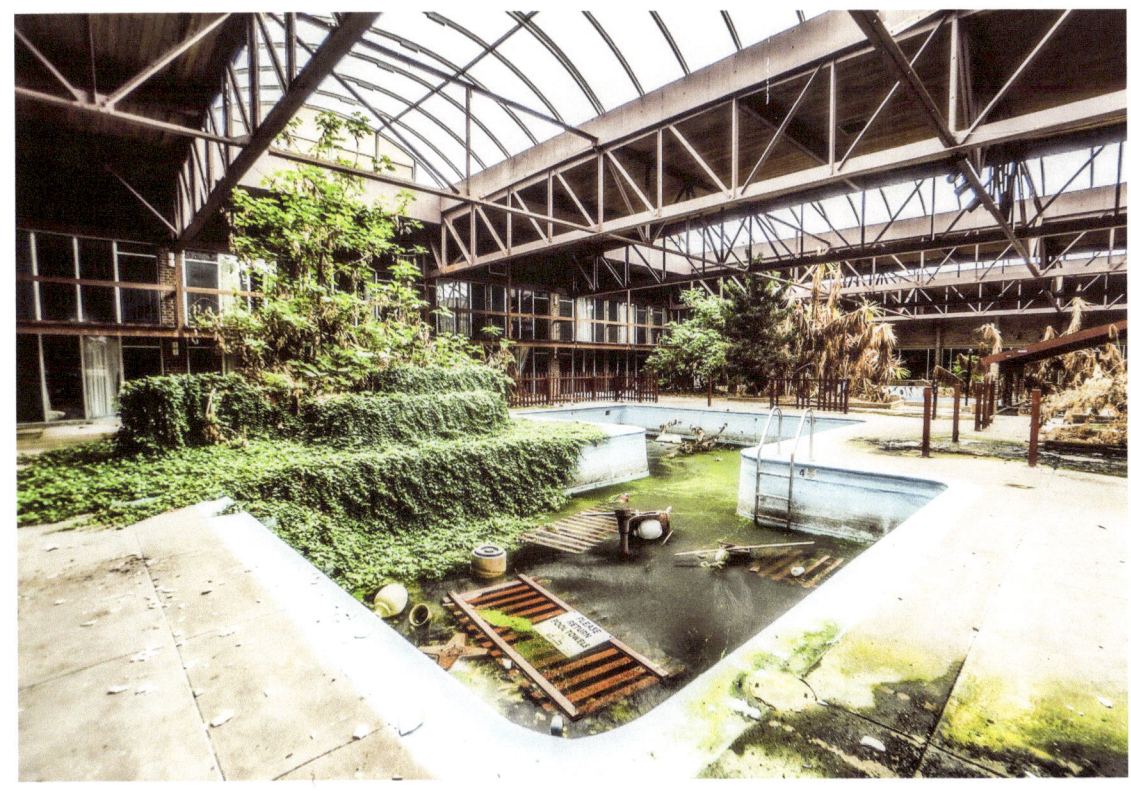

Detroit, MI

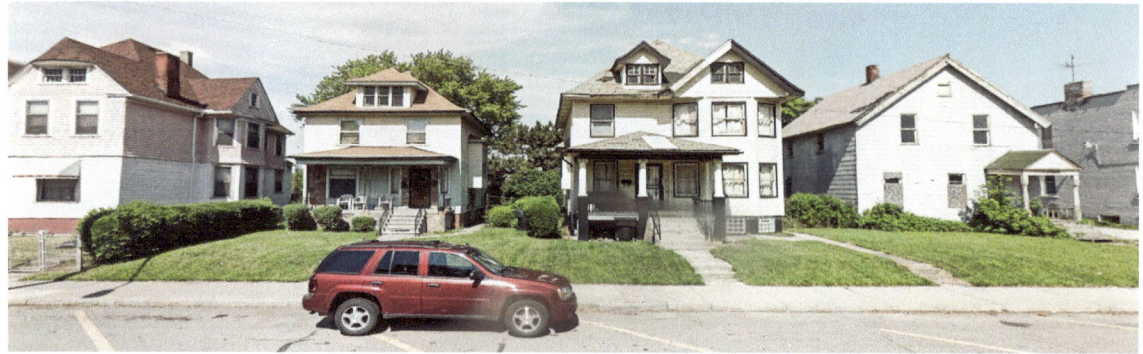

June 2011

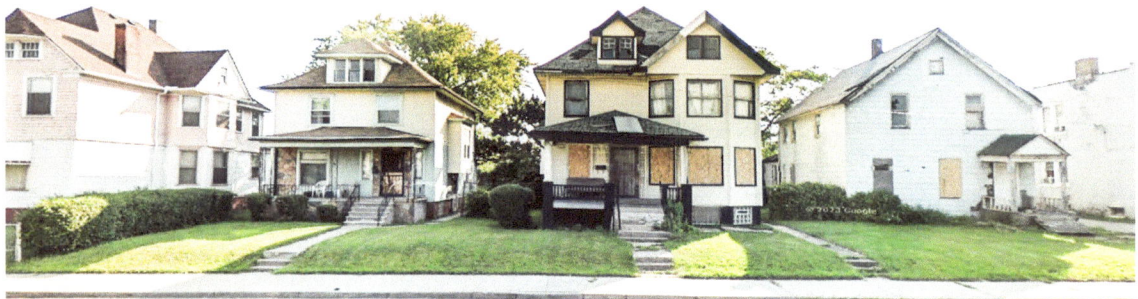

September 2013

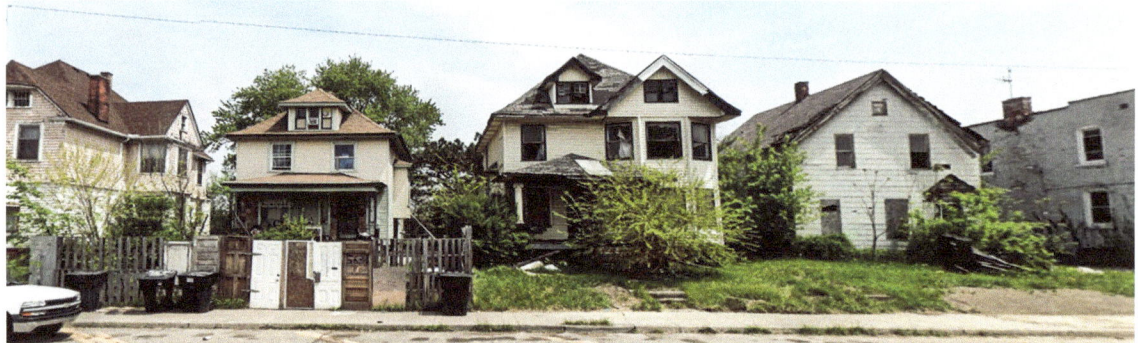

August 2018

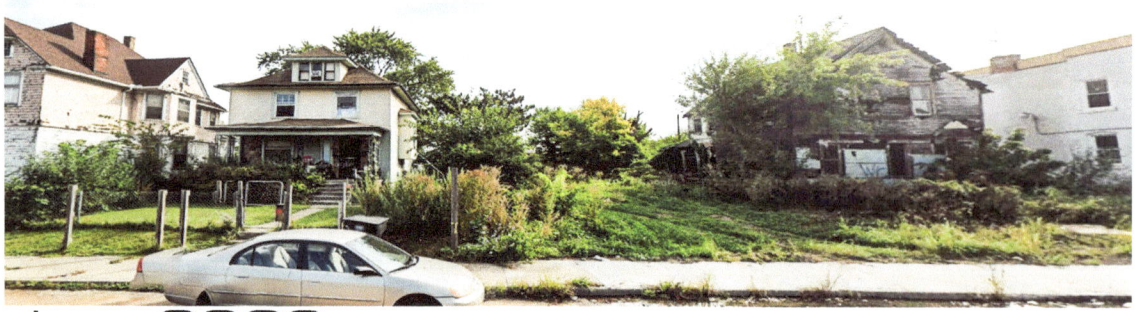

June 2023

Diamonds Restaurant - Missouri

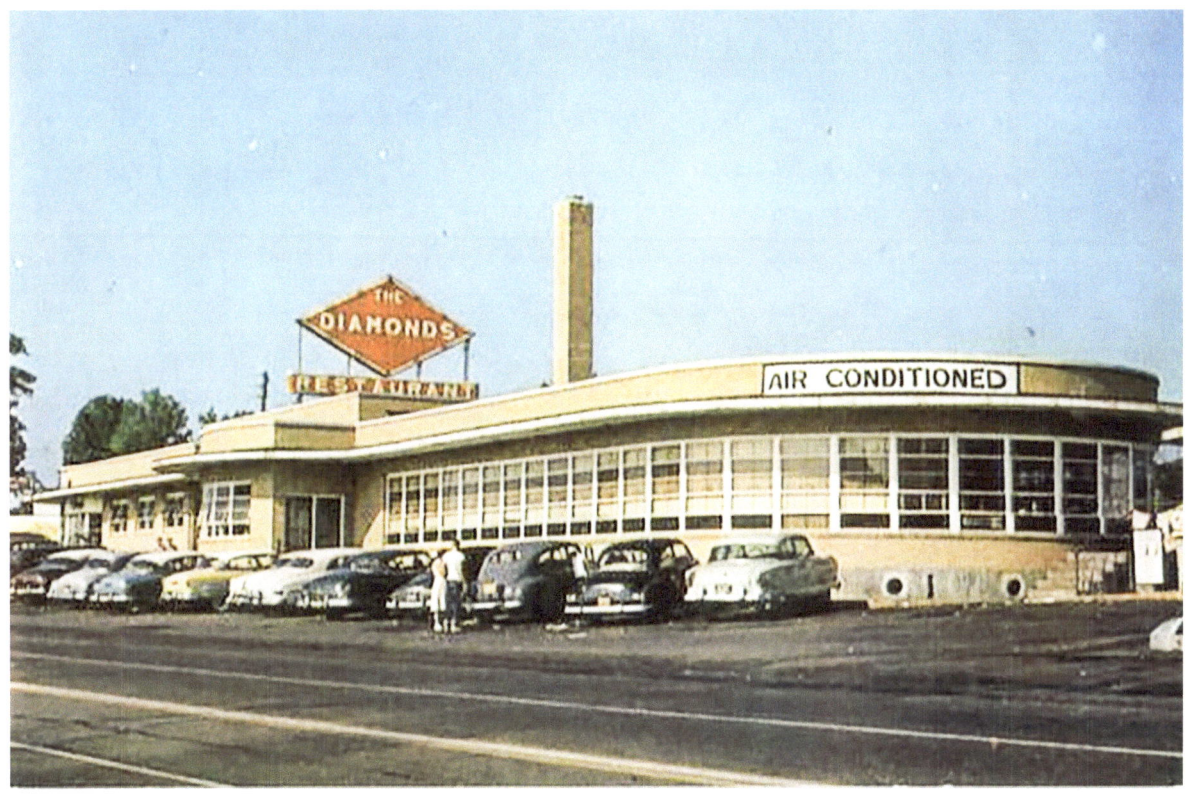

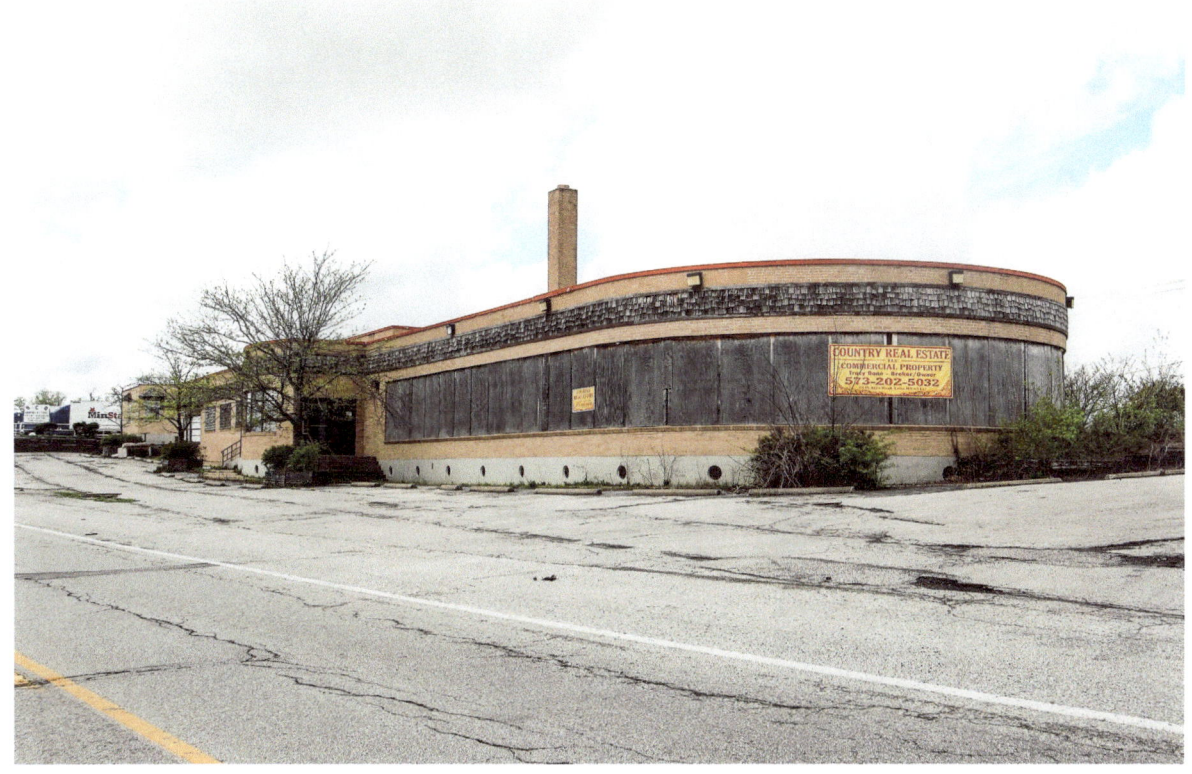

Fix-it-Shop Station - Texola, OK

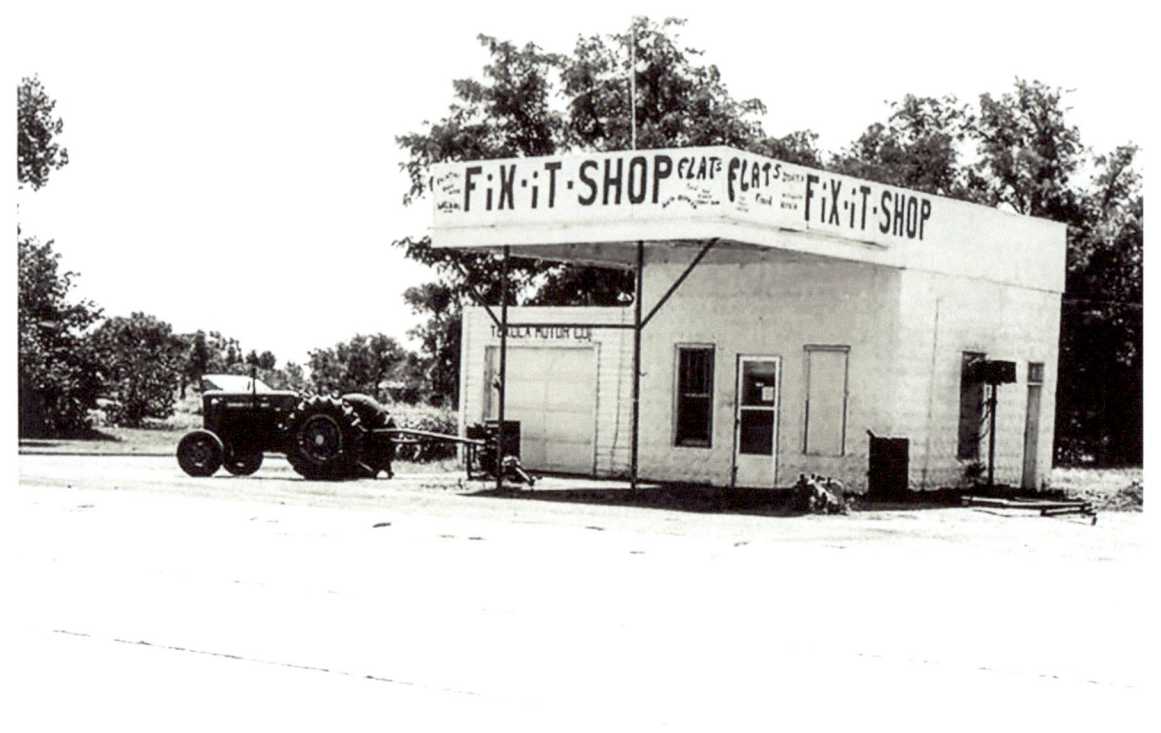

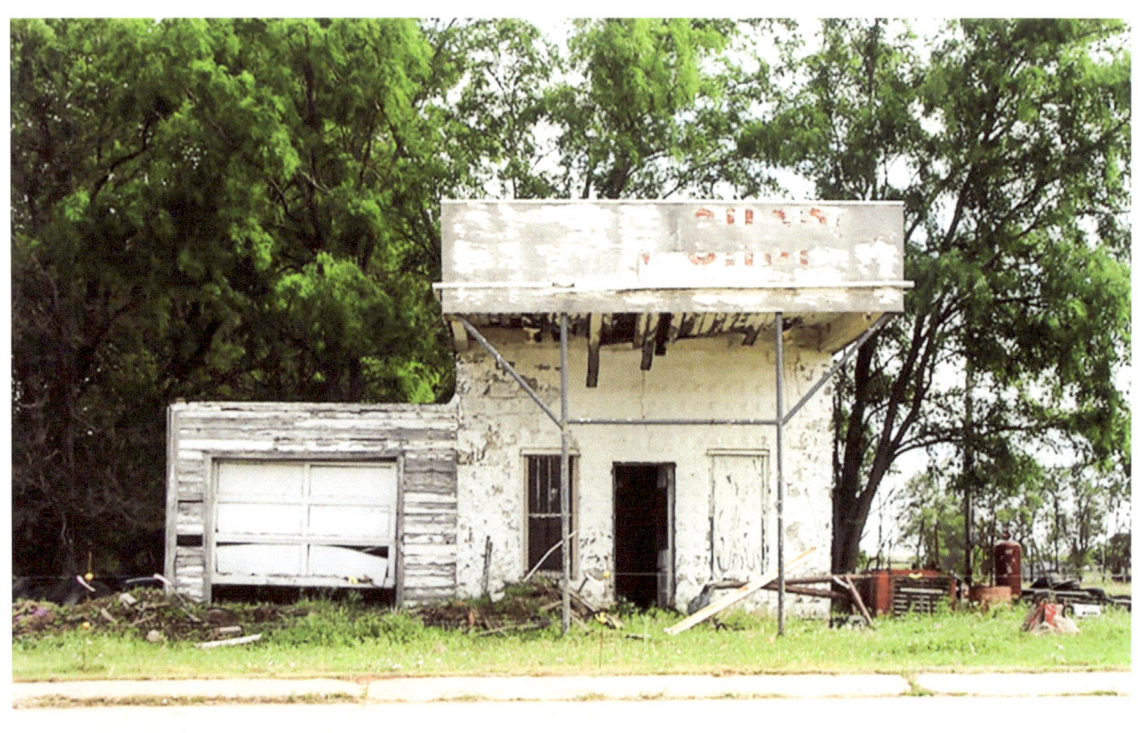

Griffith Park Zoo - Los Angeles, CA

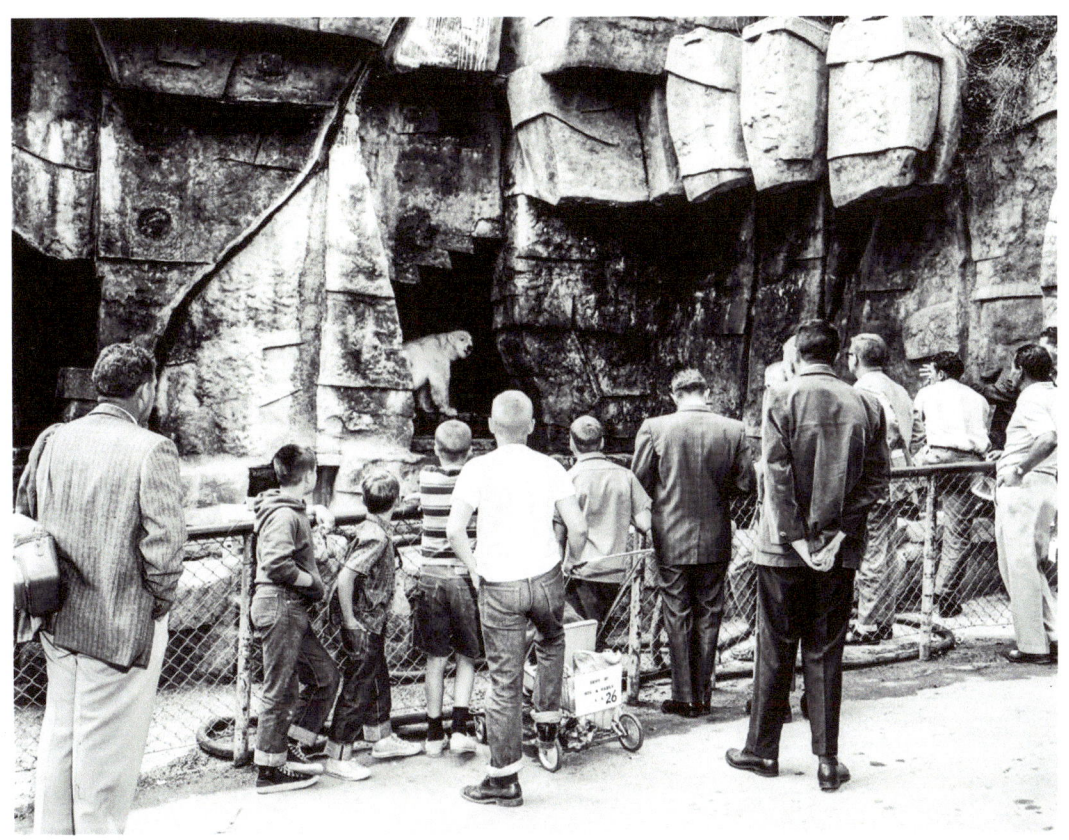

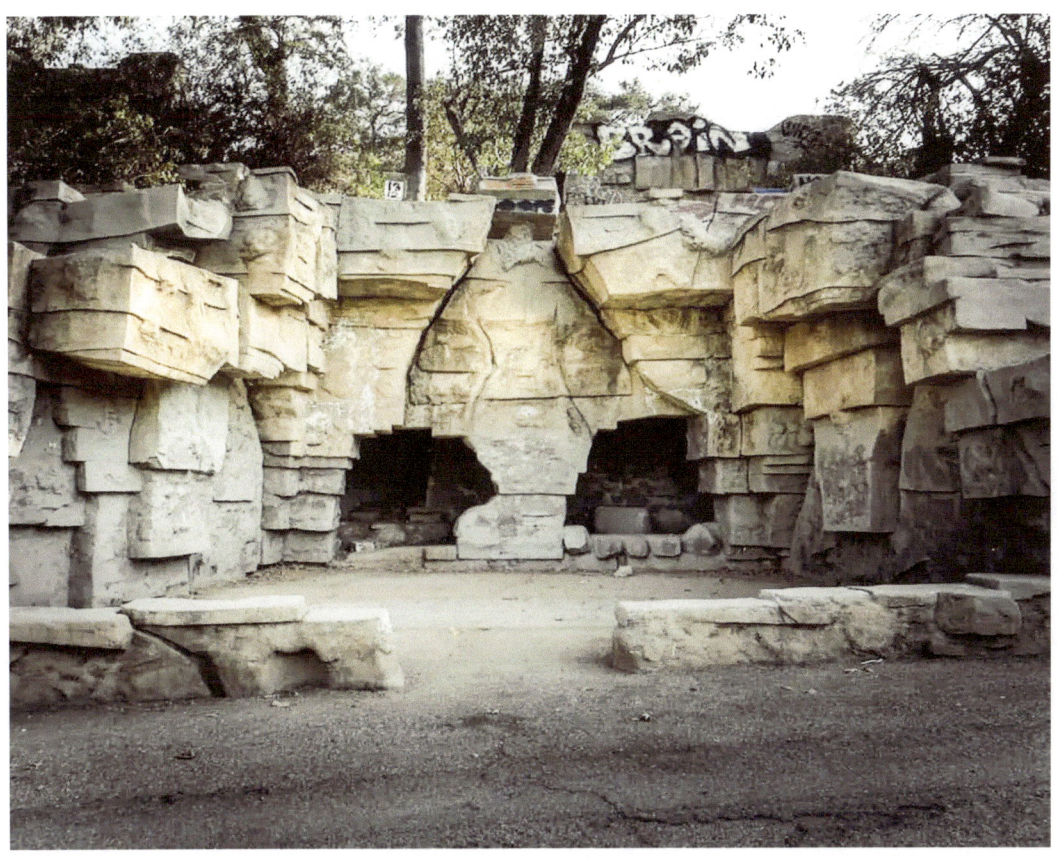

Mansion - Detroit, Michigan

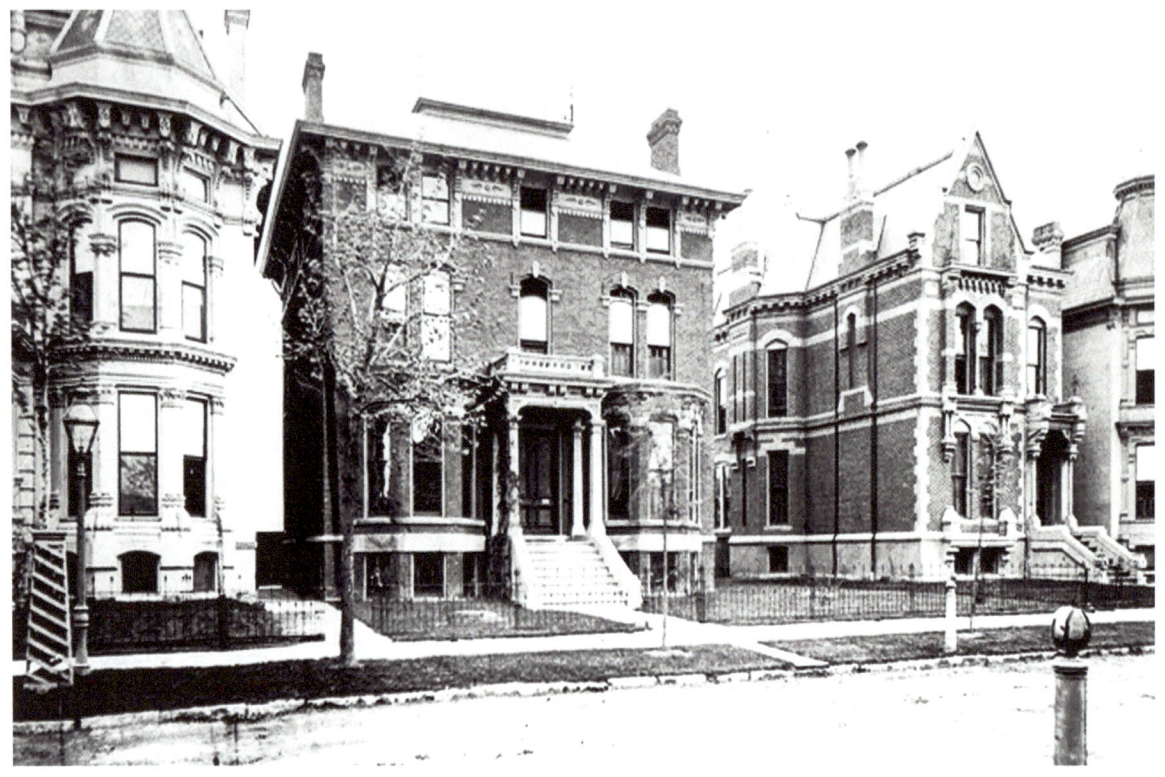

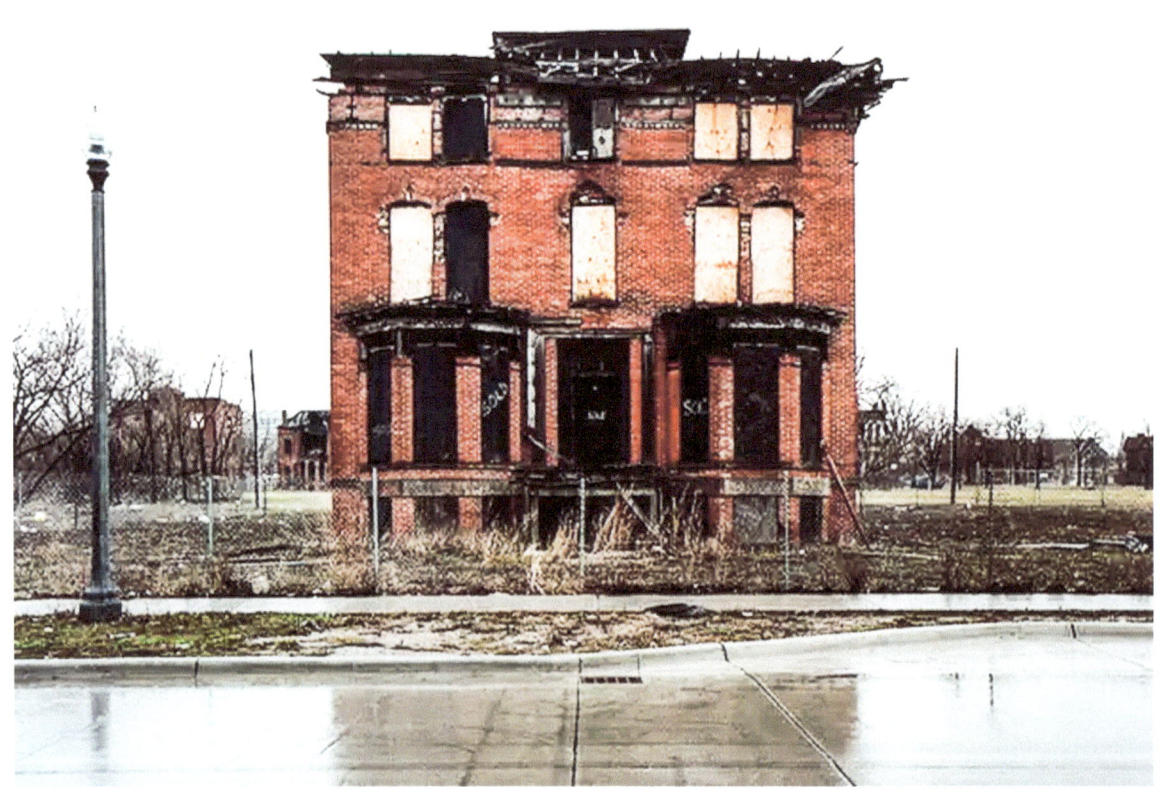

Grossinger's Resort Outdoor Pool - NY

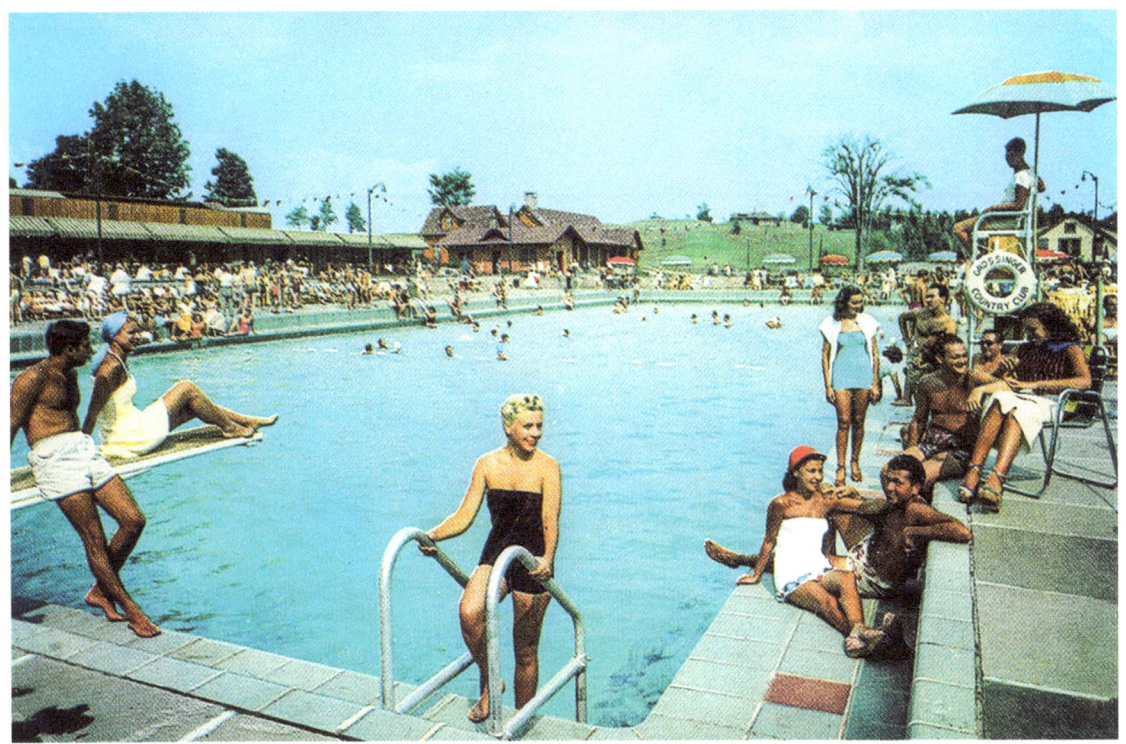

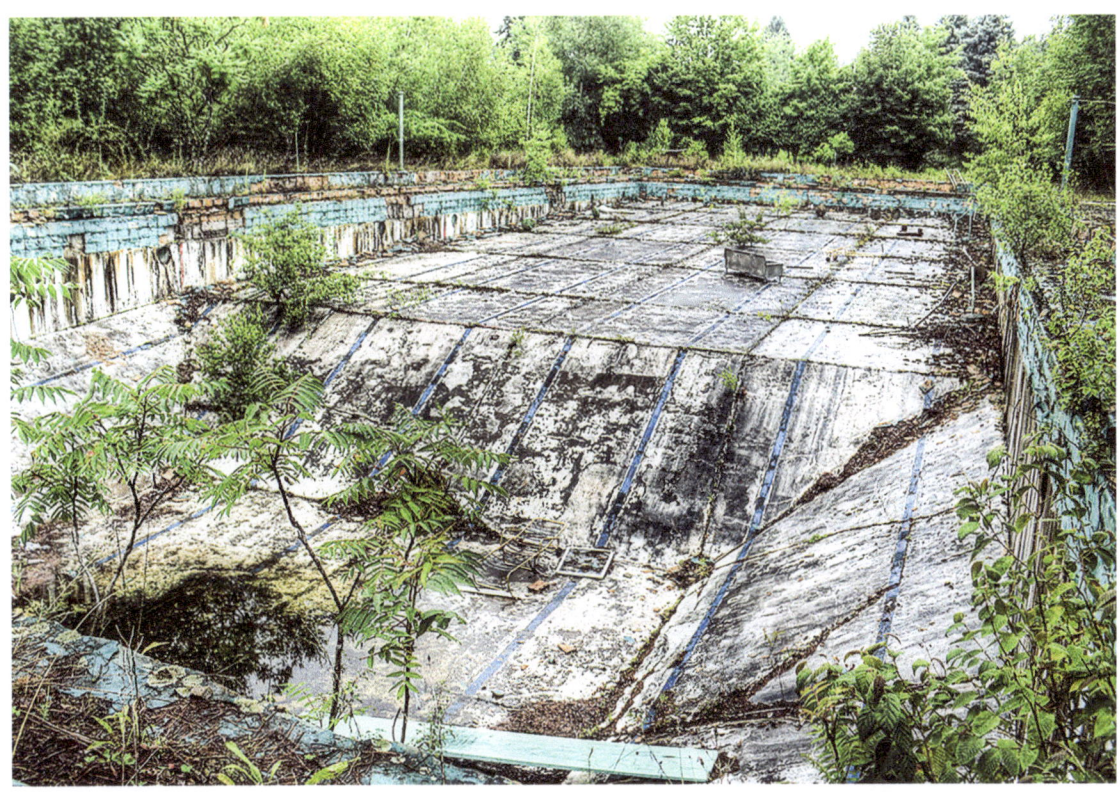

Houston Astrodome - Houston, TX

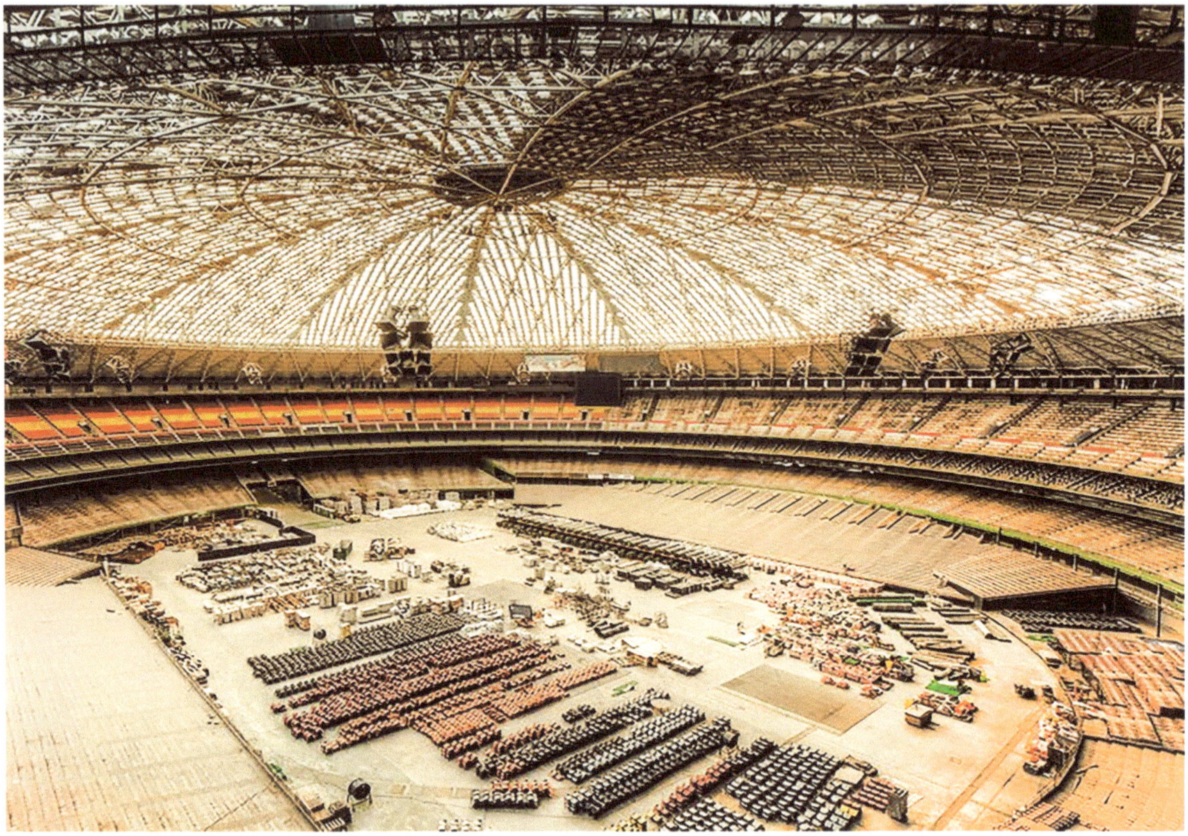

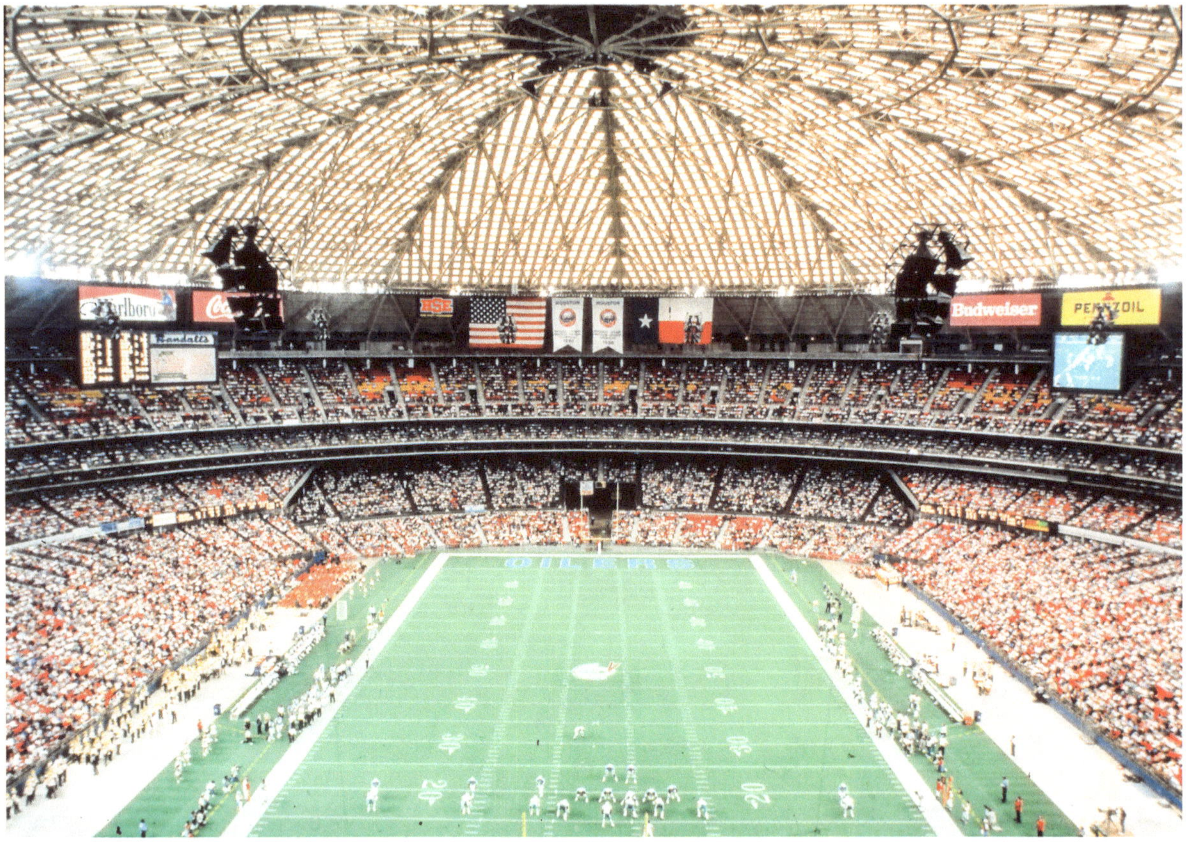

Wild Waters Park - Silver Springs, FL

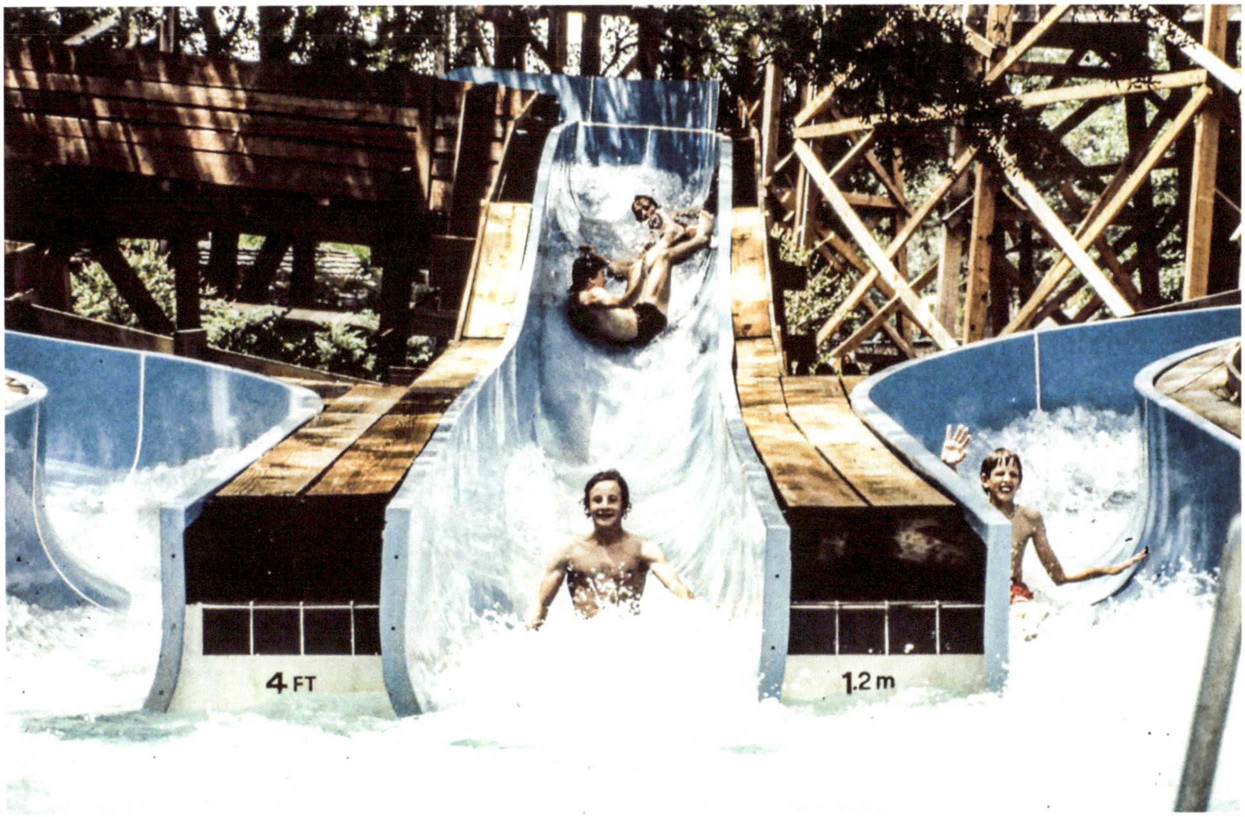

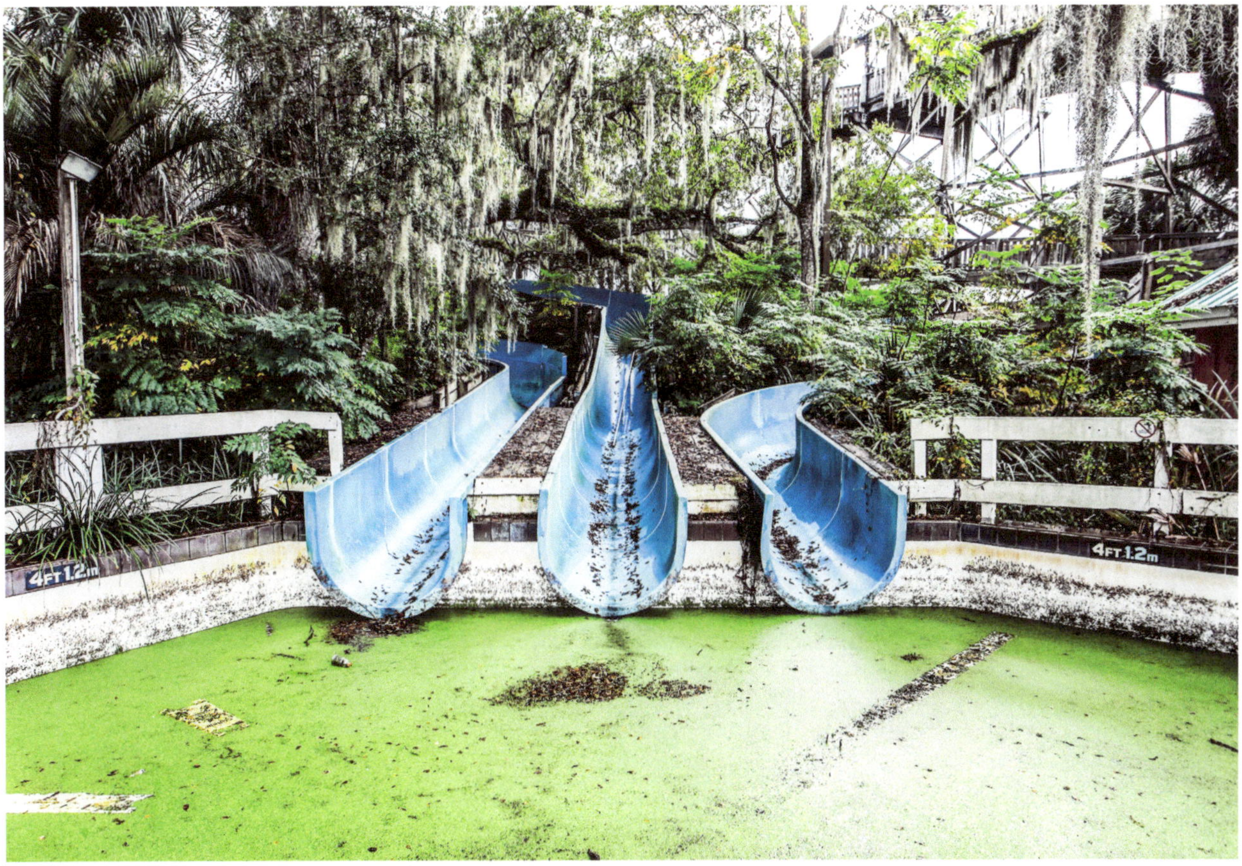

McDonald's "McBarge" - Vancouver, Canada

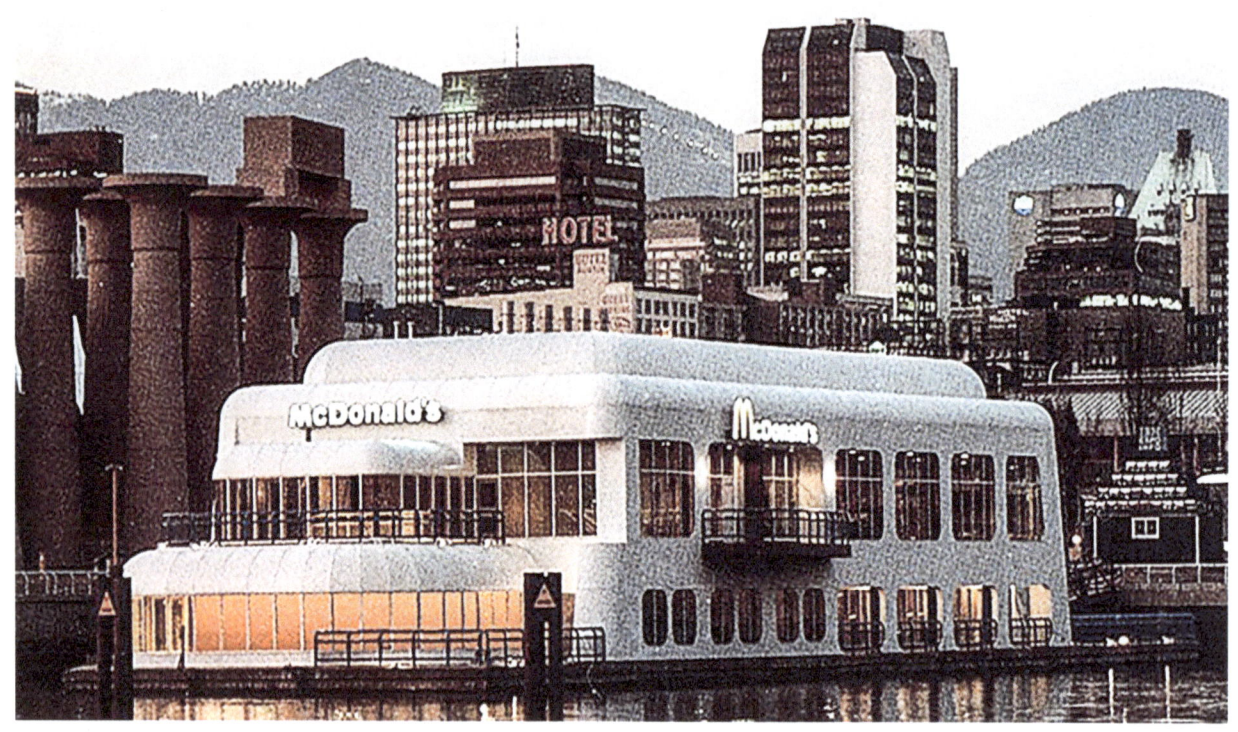

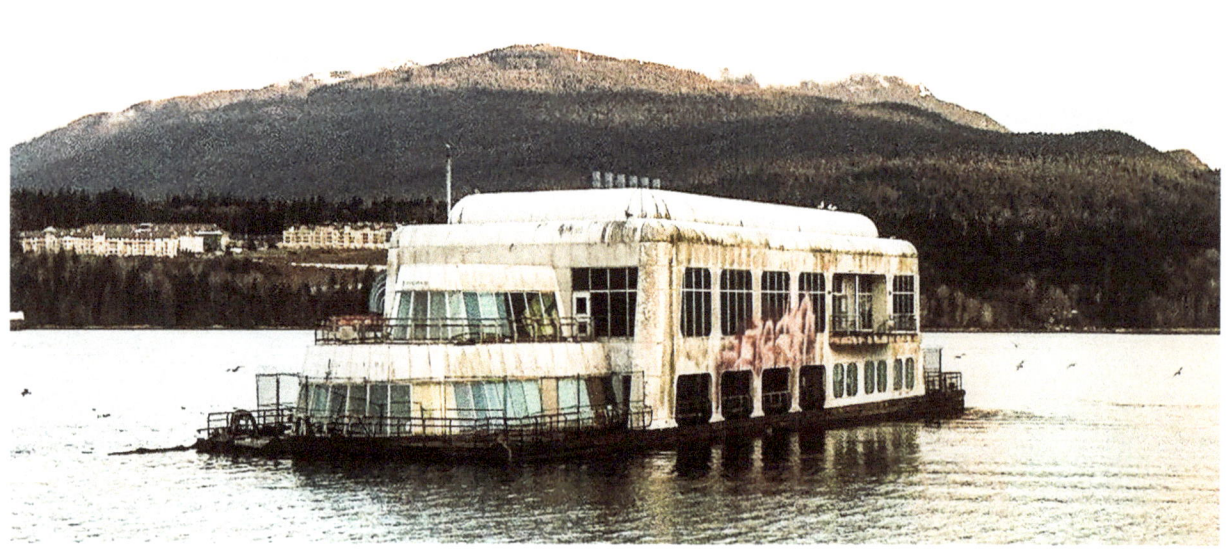

The Robert E. Lee Motel - Bristol, Virginia

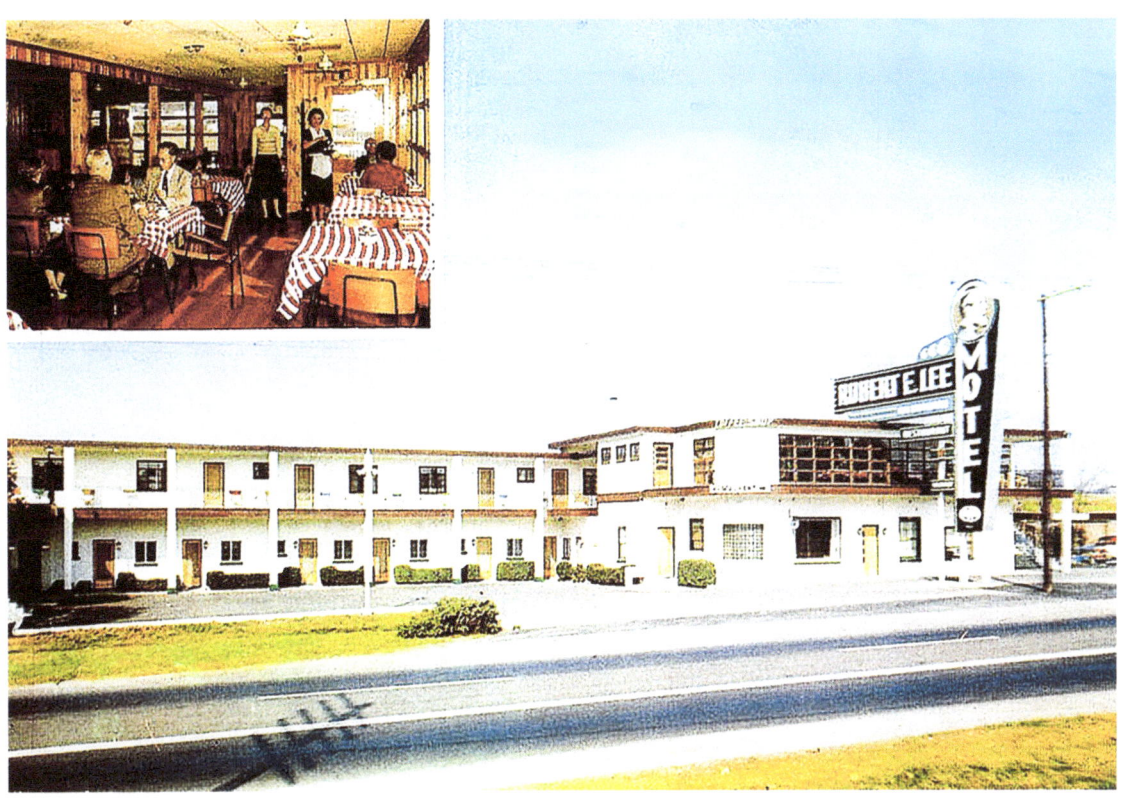

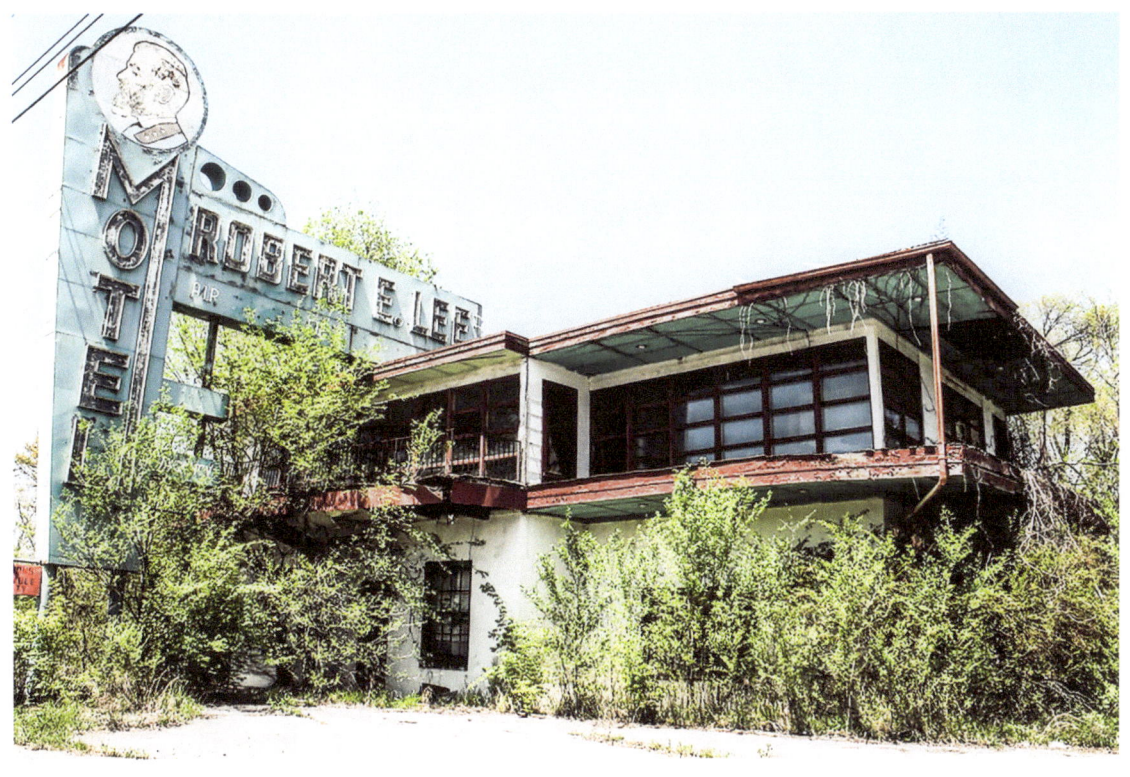

Minden Auto - Carson City, NV

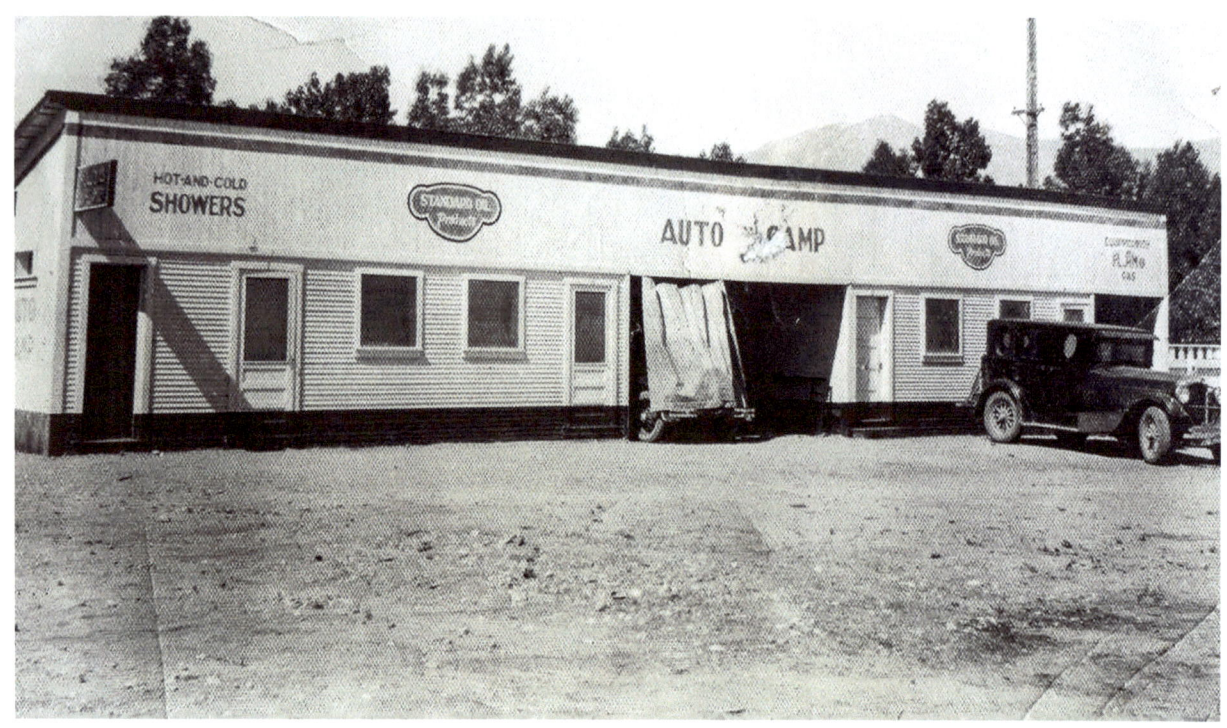

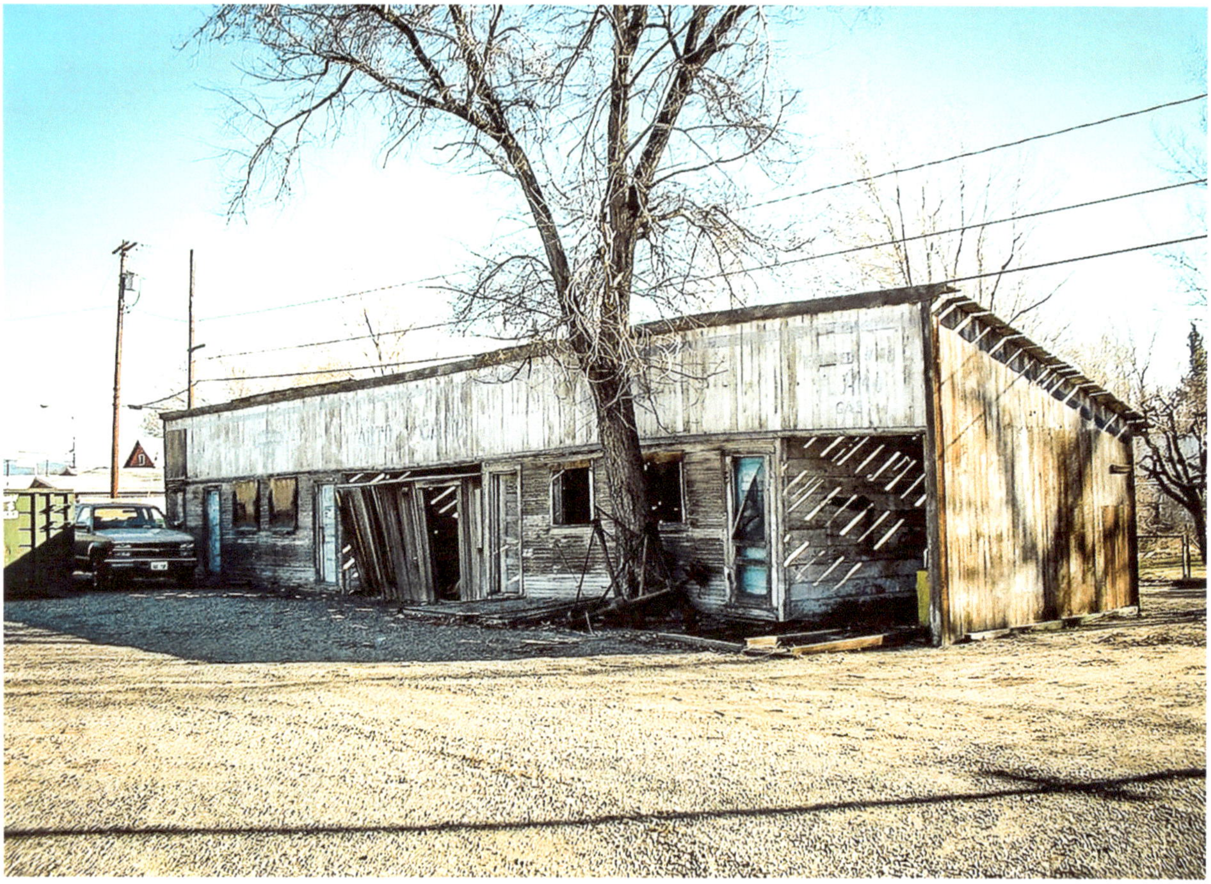

The Mirante Belvedere restaurant - Rio de Janeiro

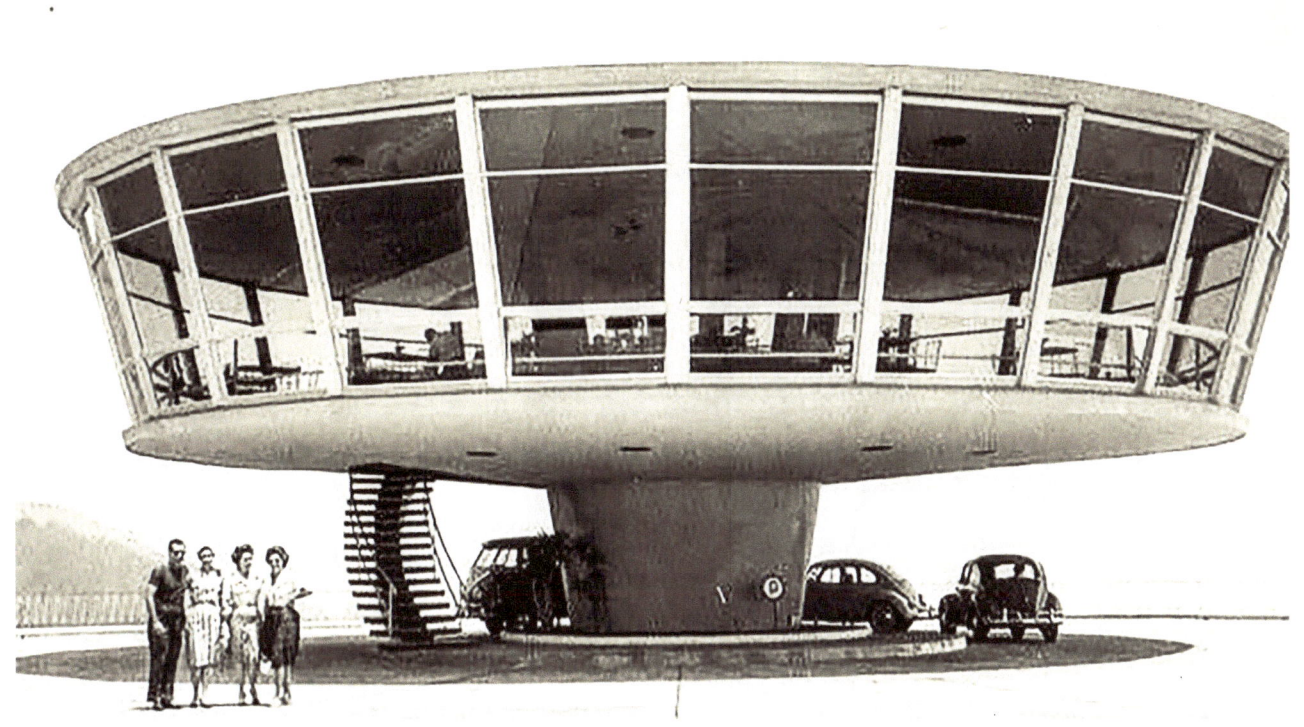

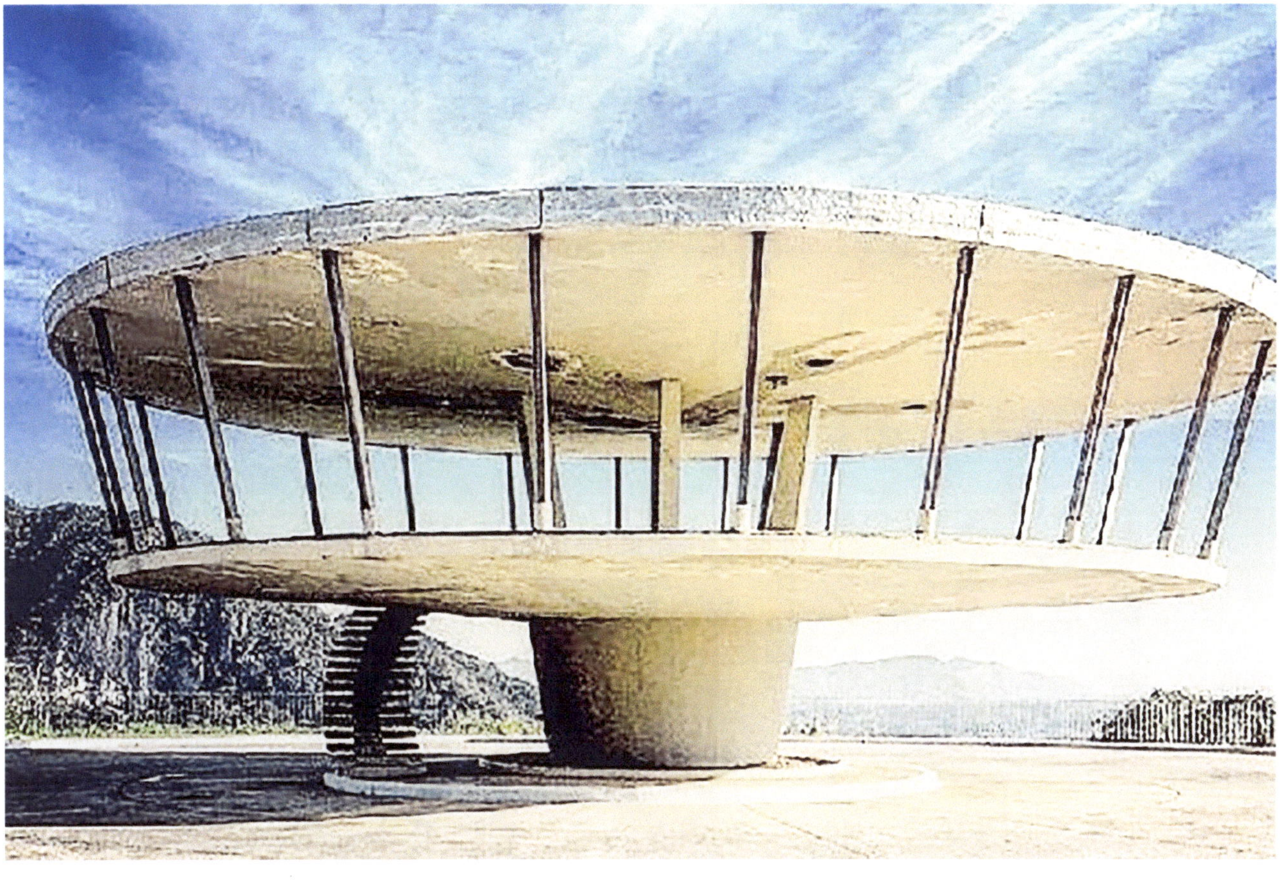

Nicosia International Airport - Cyprus

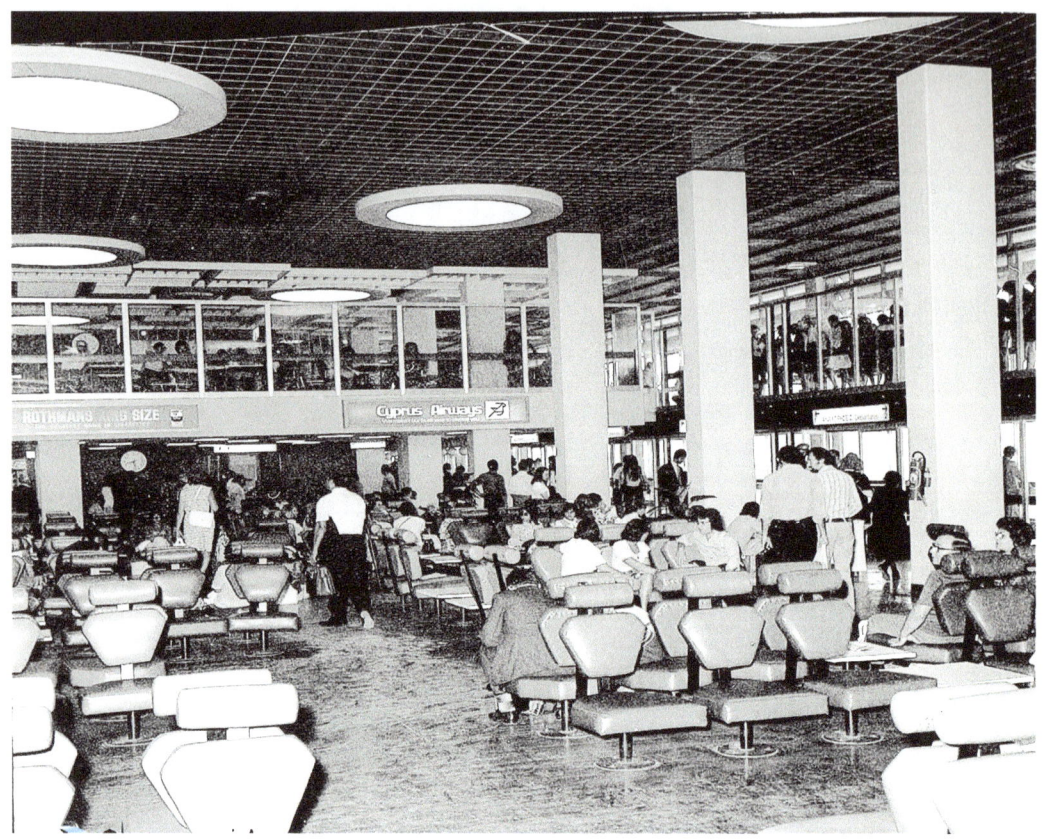

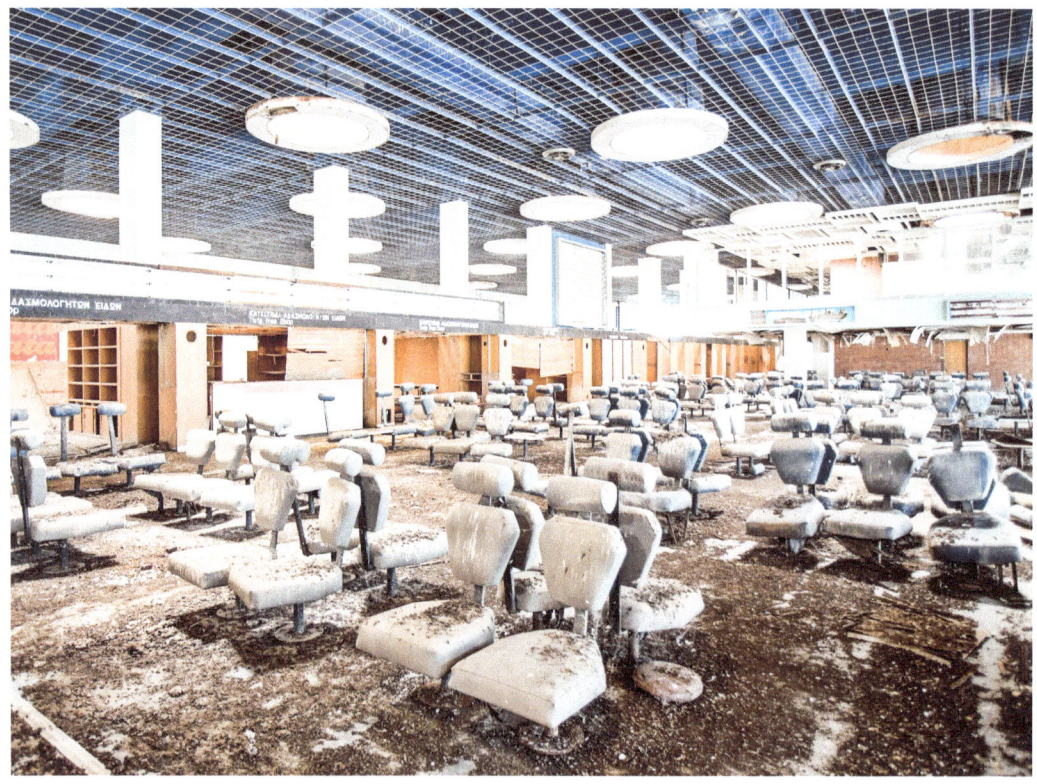

Grossinger's Tennis Club - NY

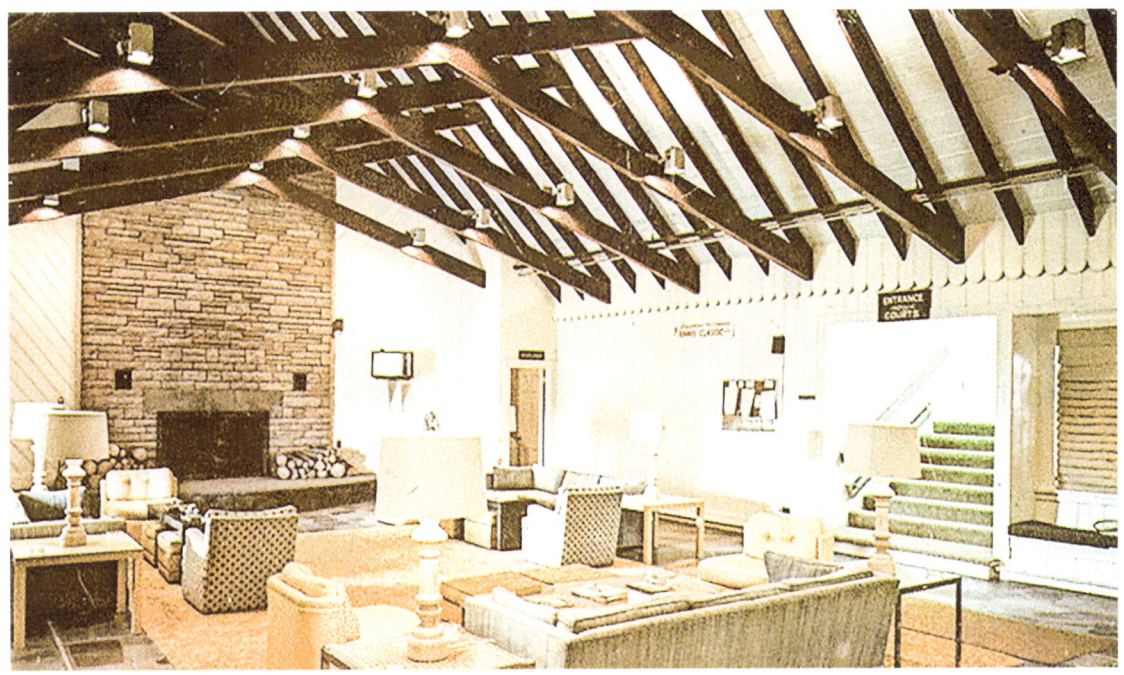

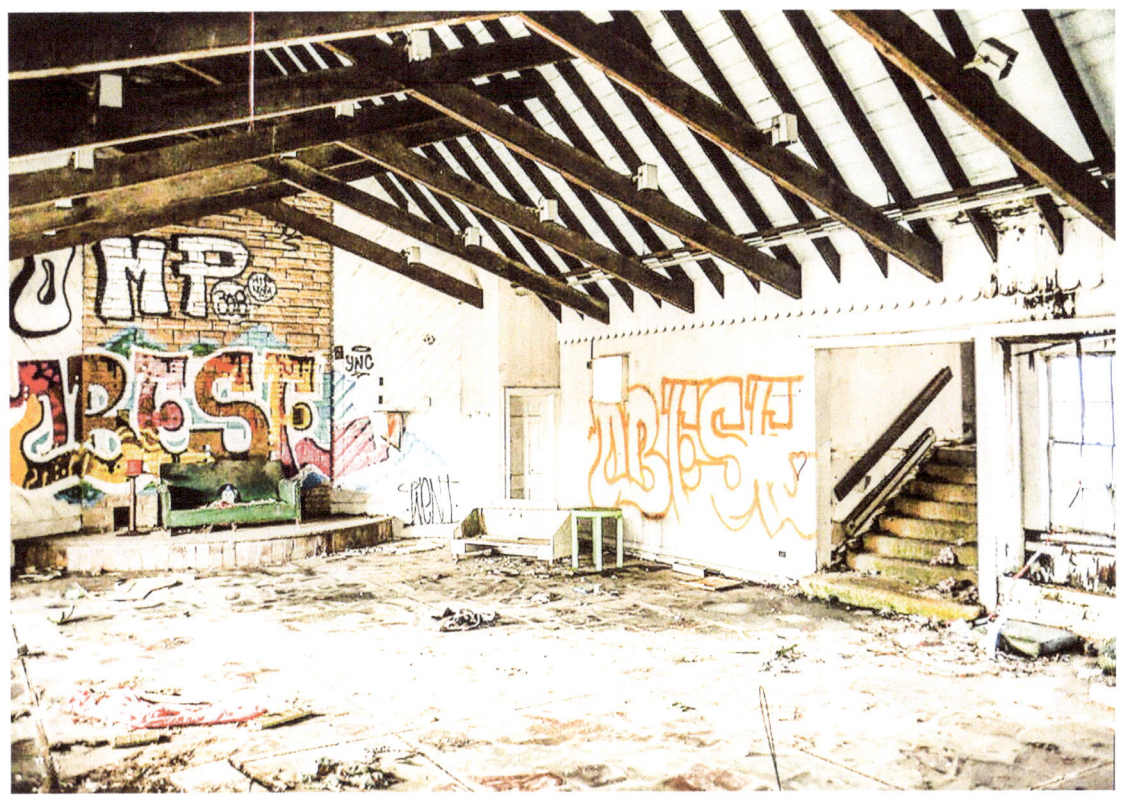

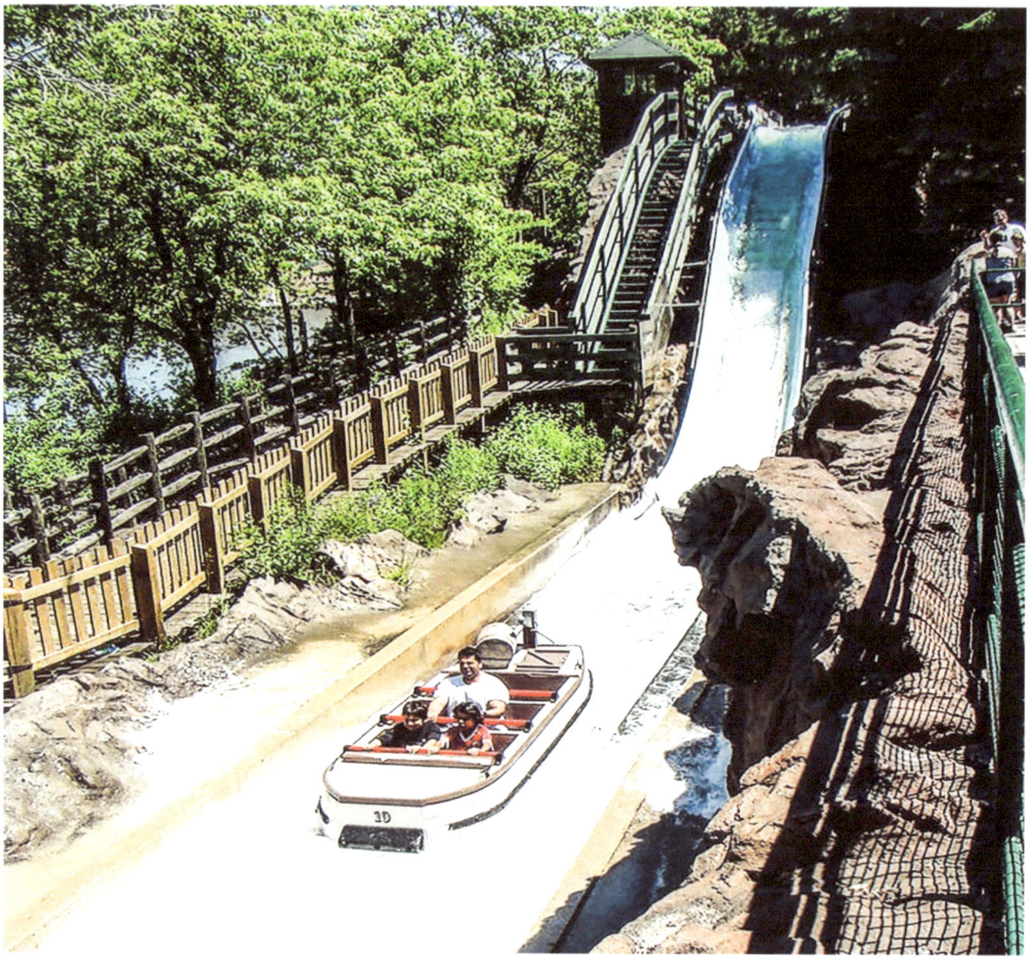

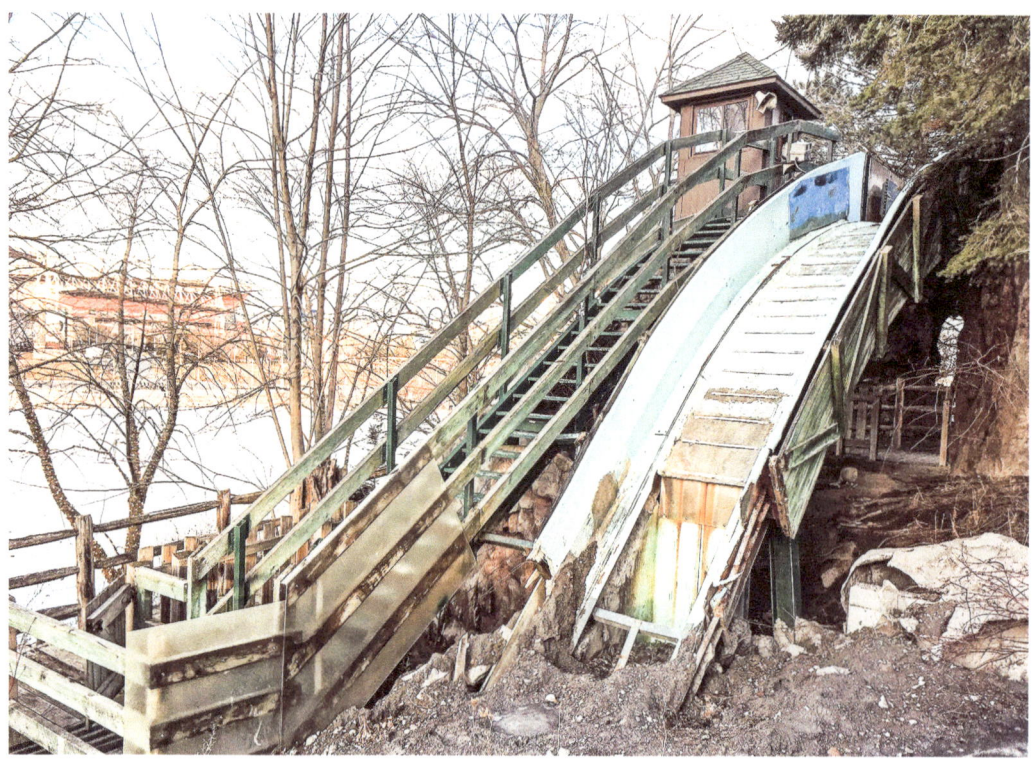

Twin Arrows Cafe & Trading Post - Arizona

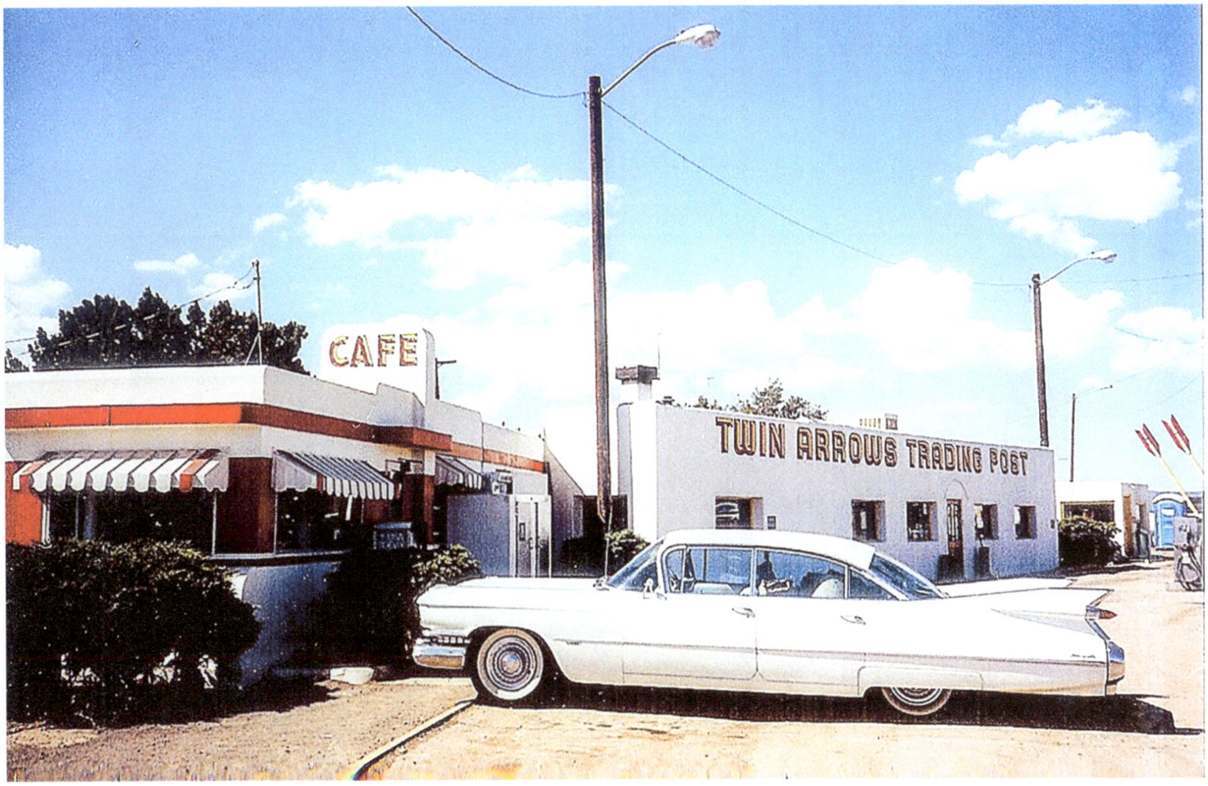

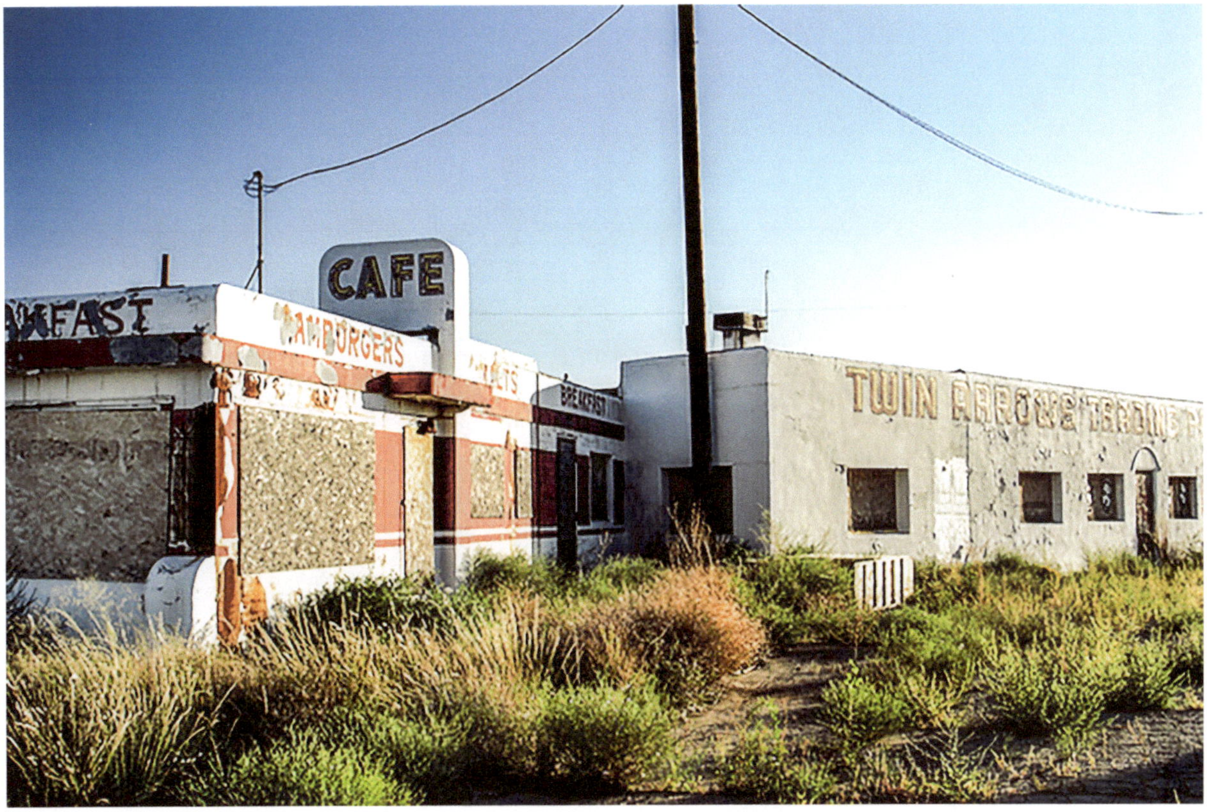

Haludovo Palace Hotel - Croatia

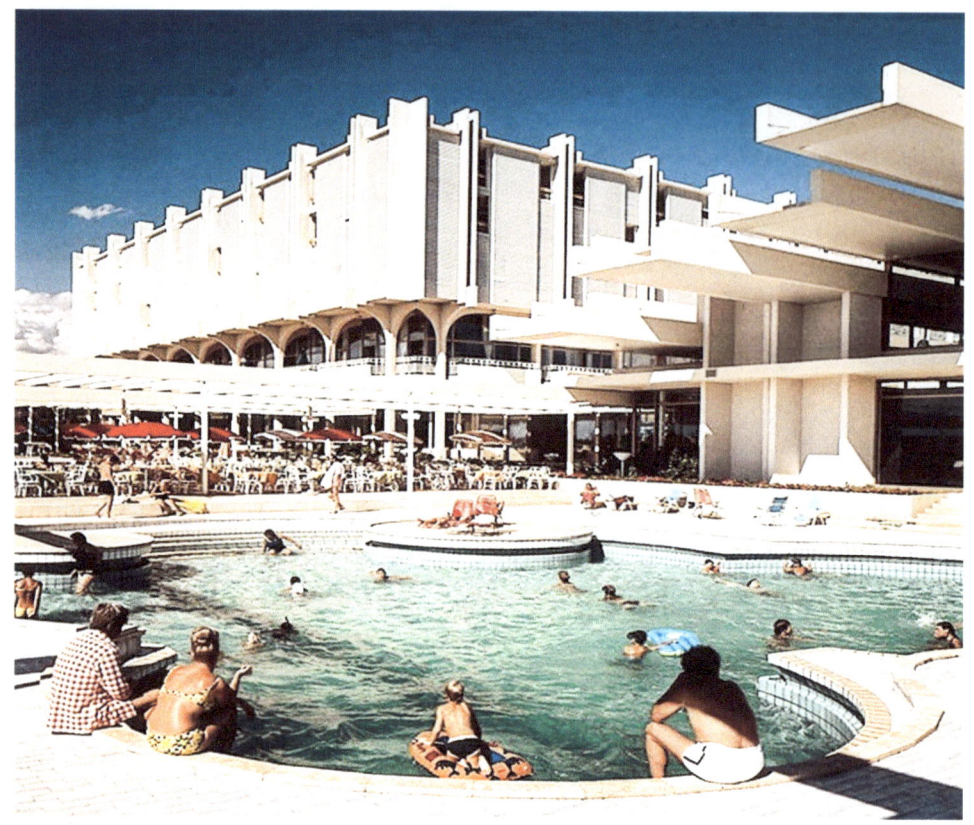

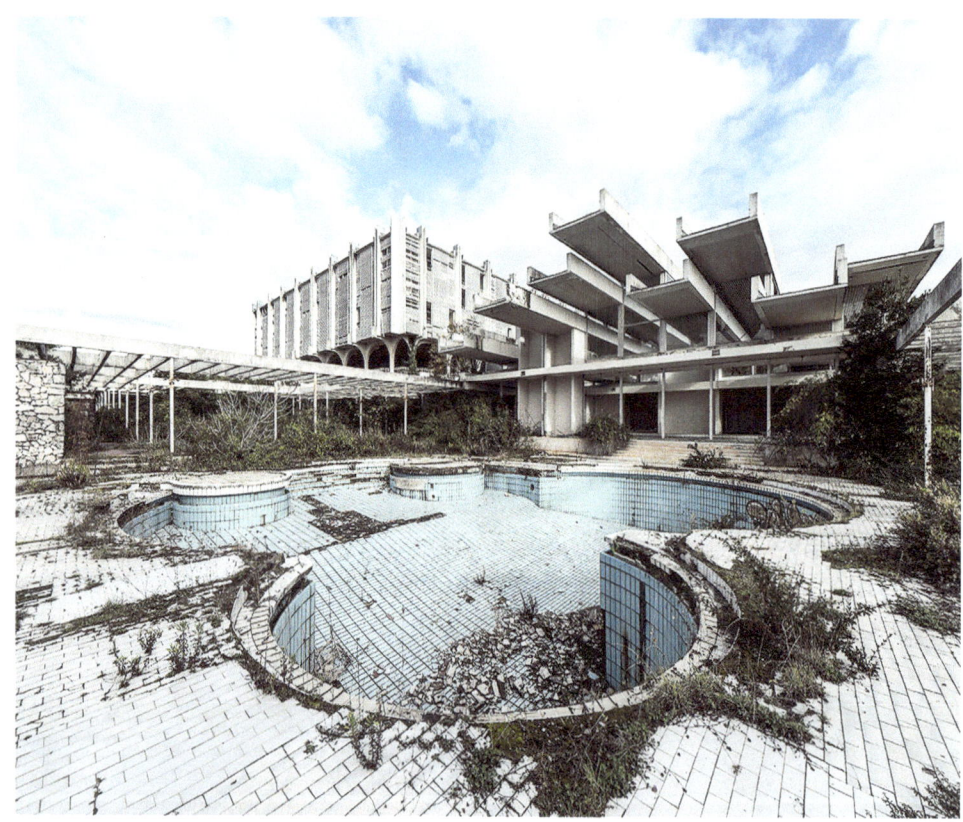

Poconos Resort - Dining Hall - NY

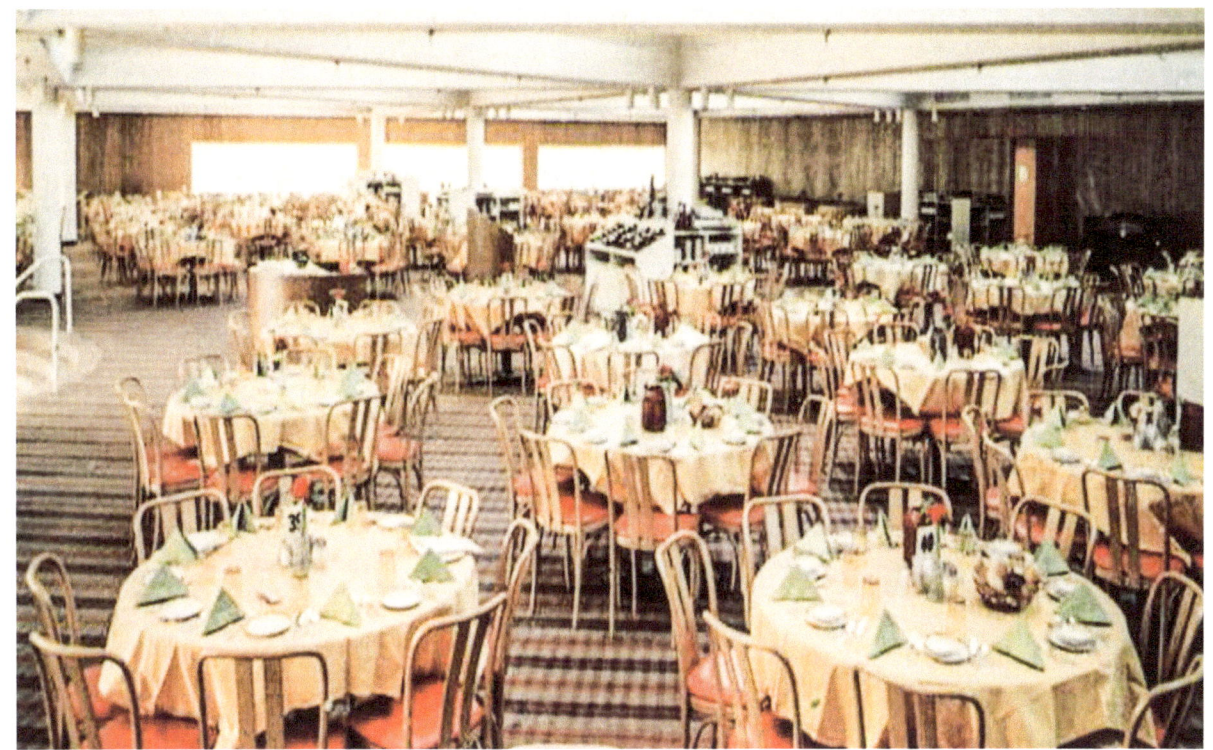

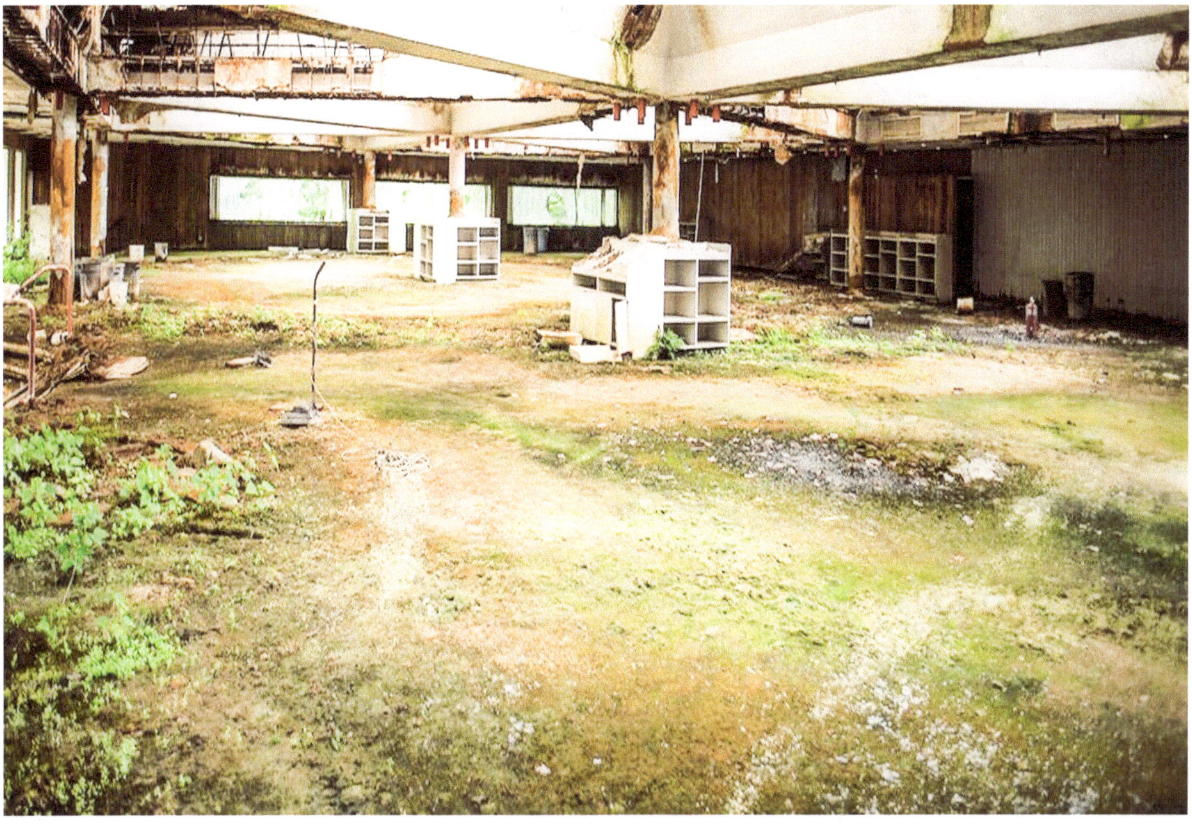

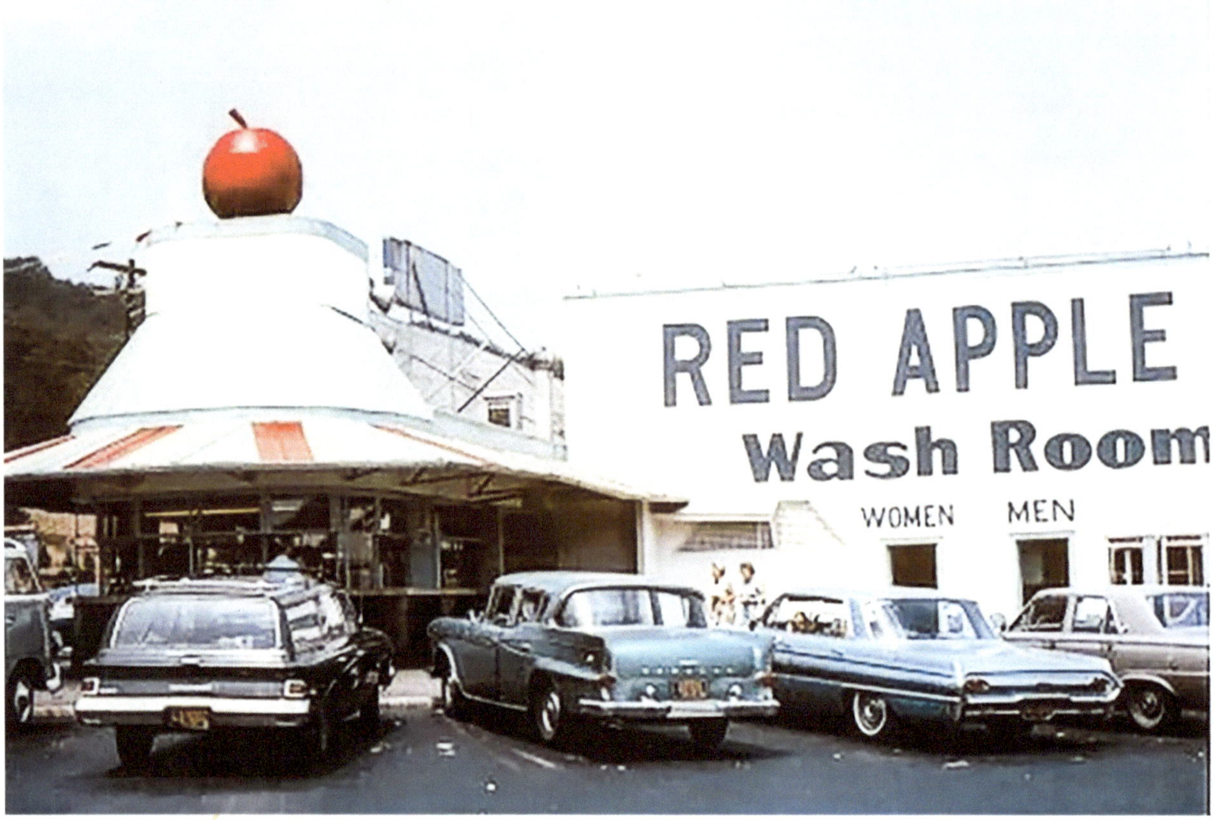

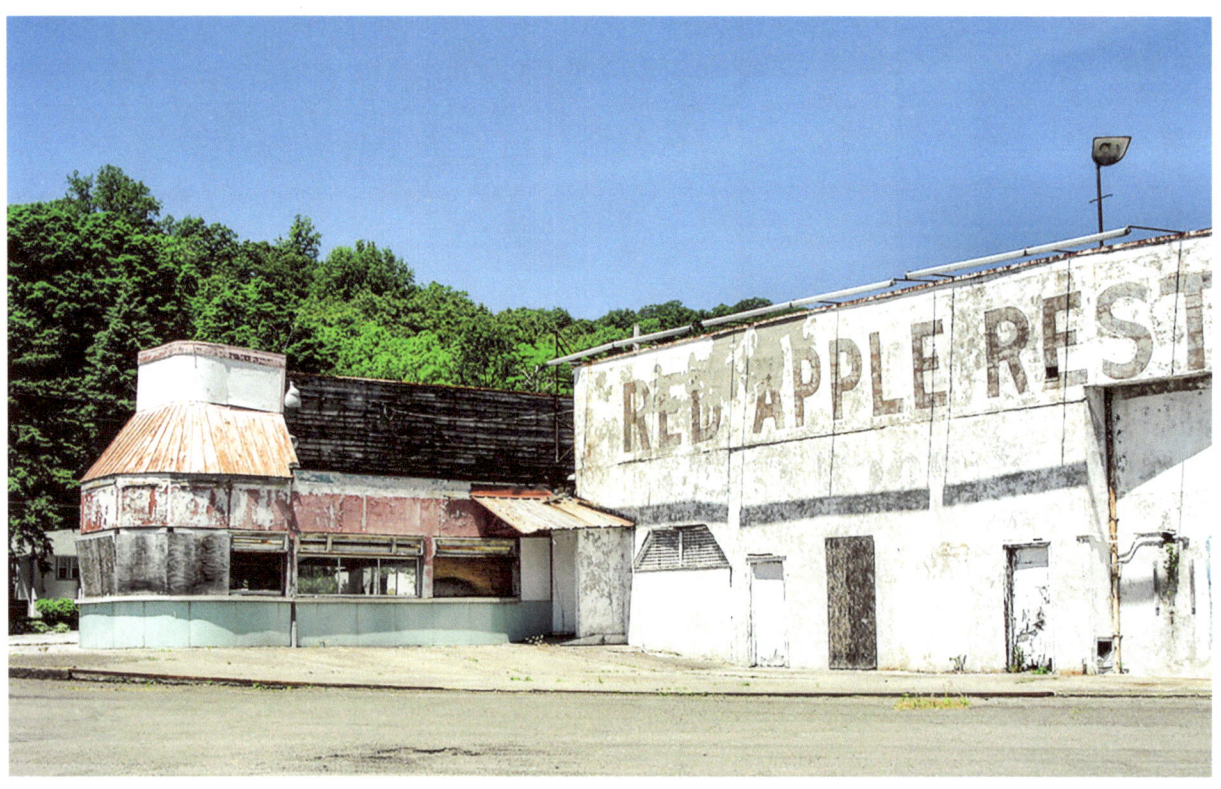

1984 Sarajevo Olympic Games Venue

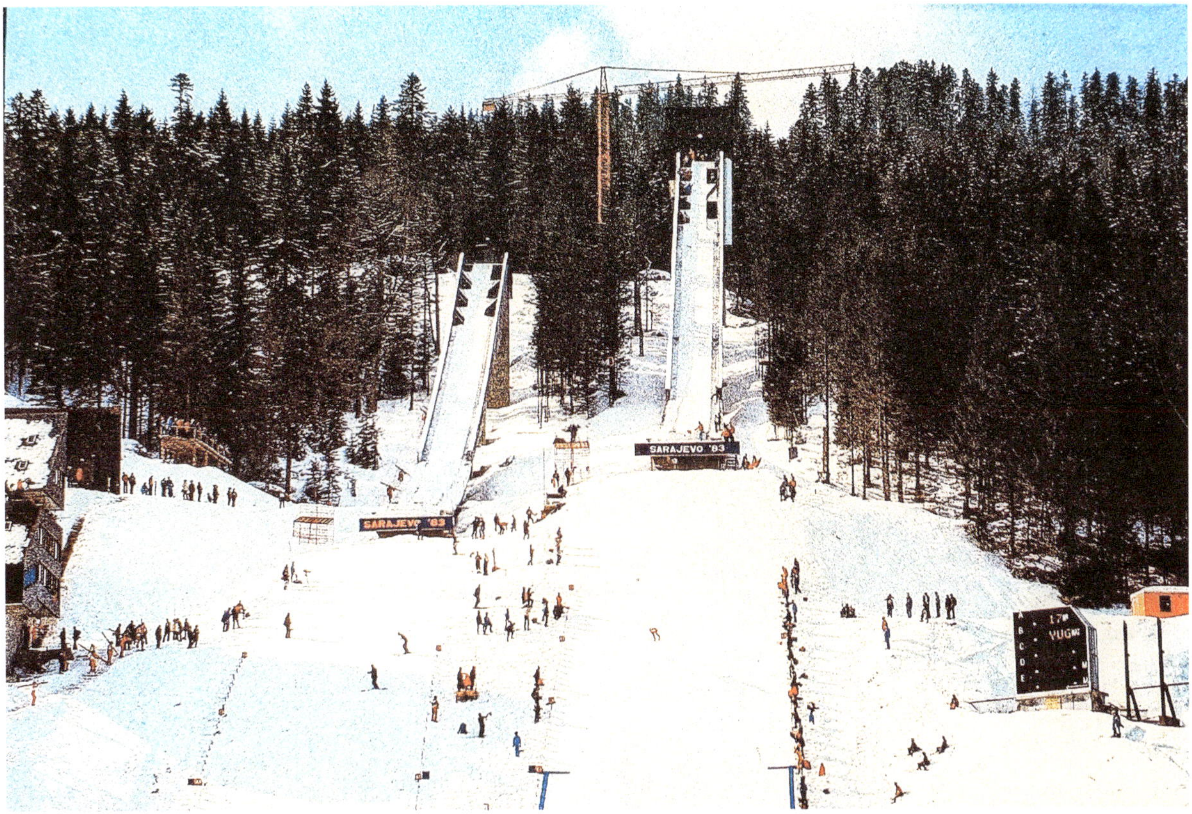

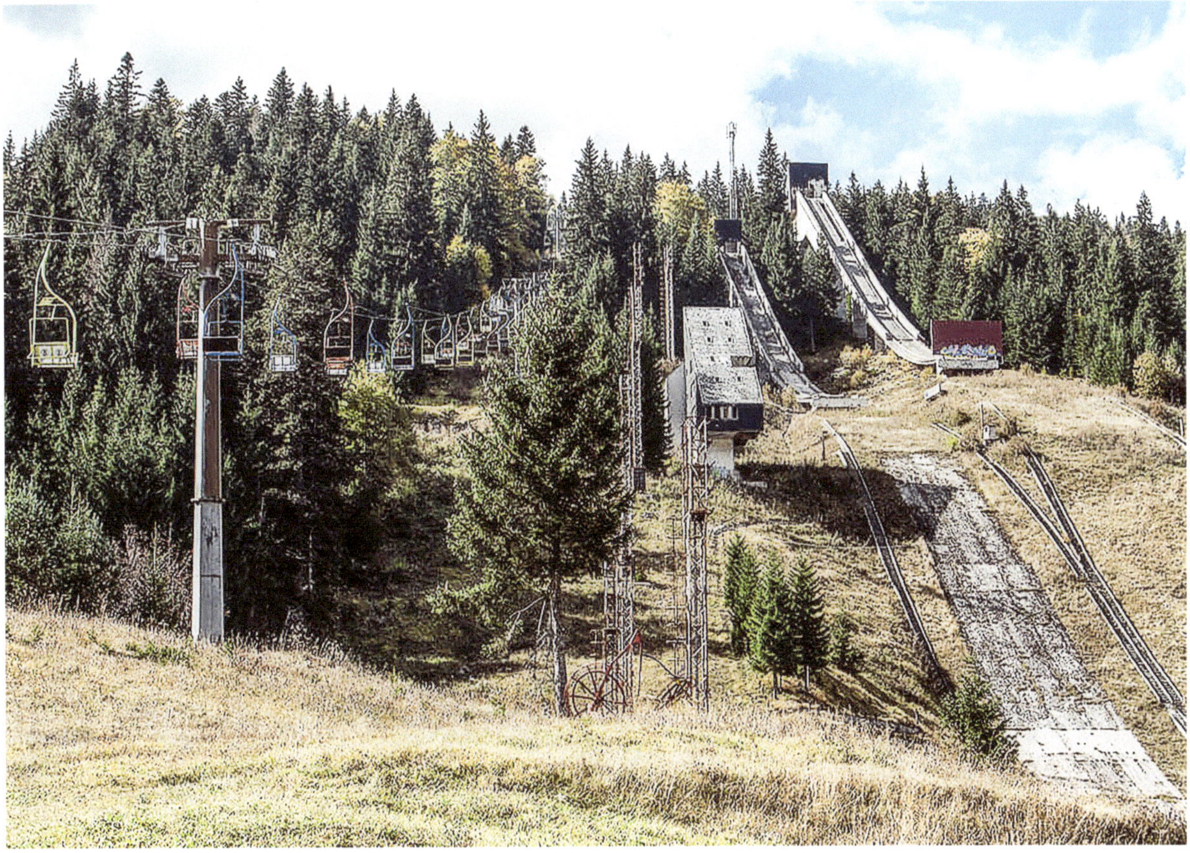

Sea-Arama - Galveston, TX

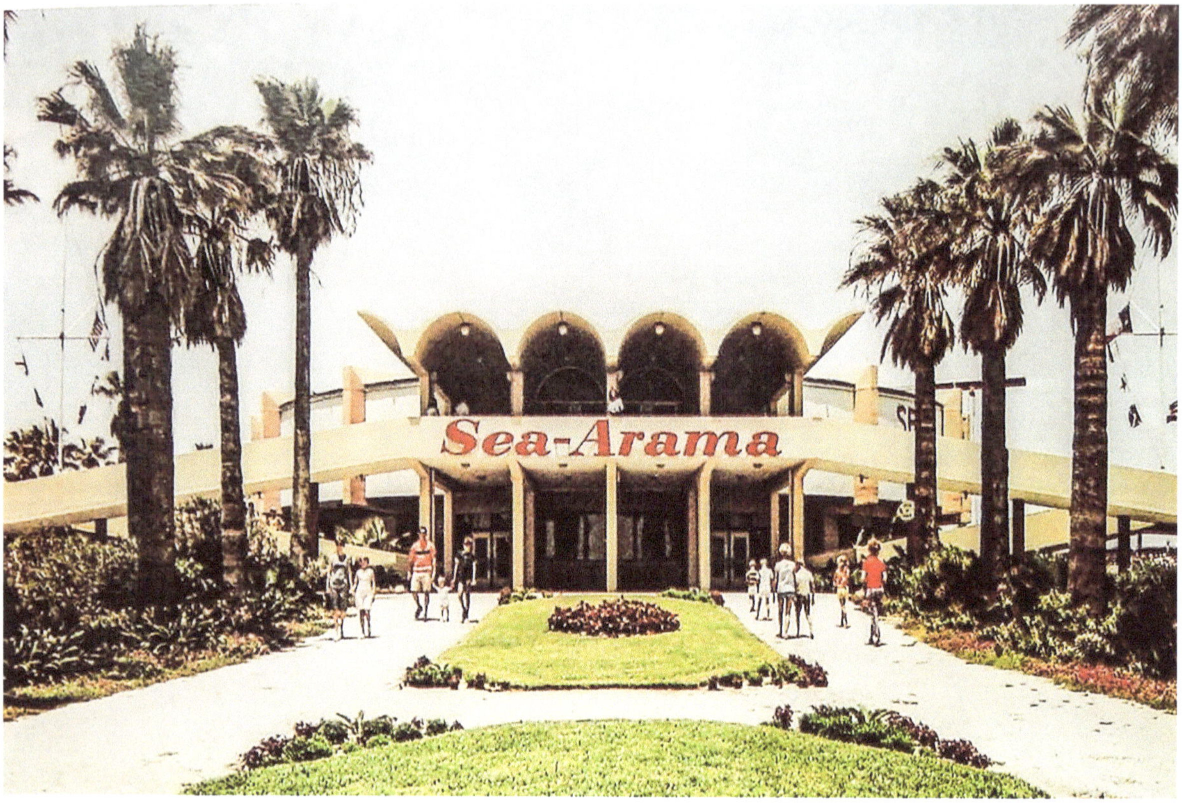

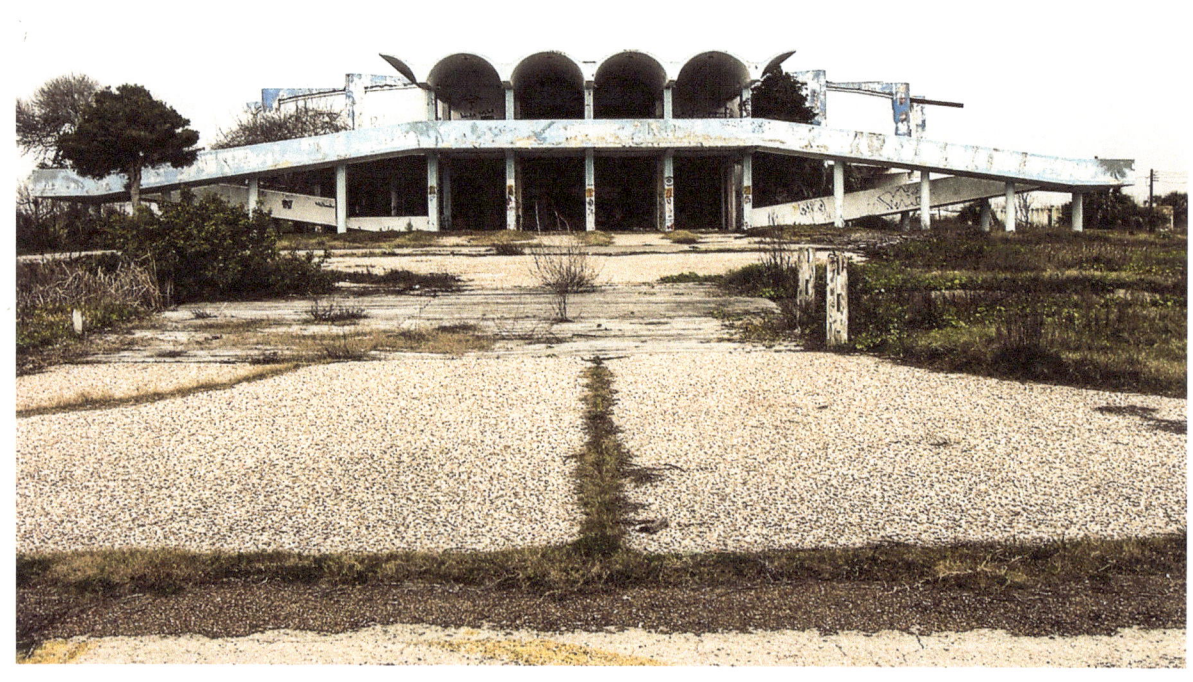

The Shack Restaurant - Snyder, TX

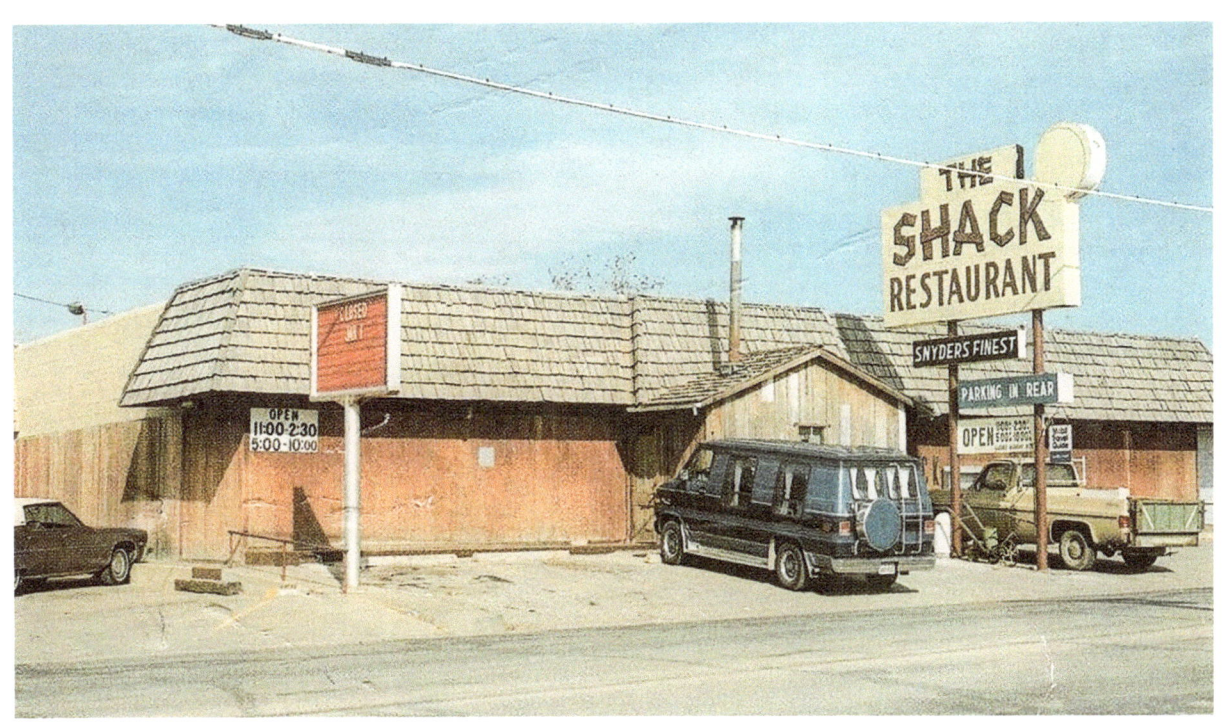

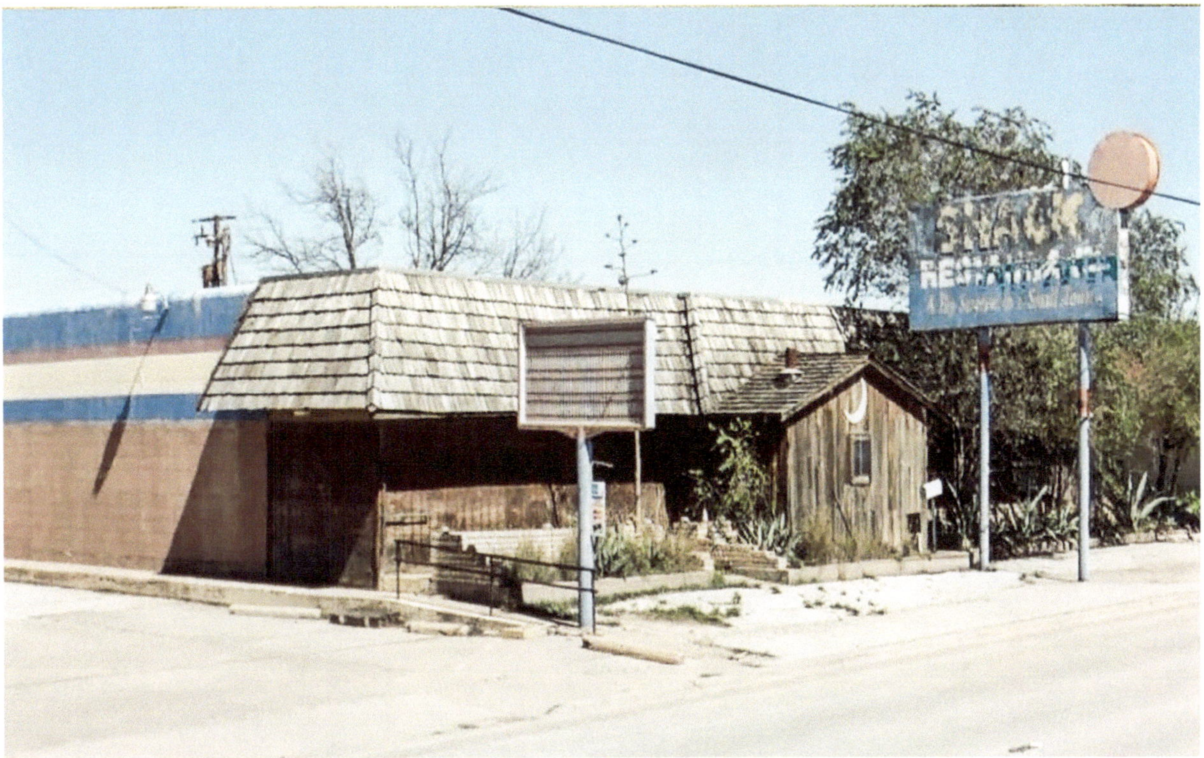

Texas World Speedway - College Station, TX

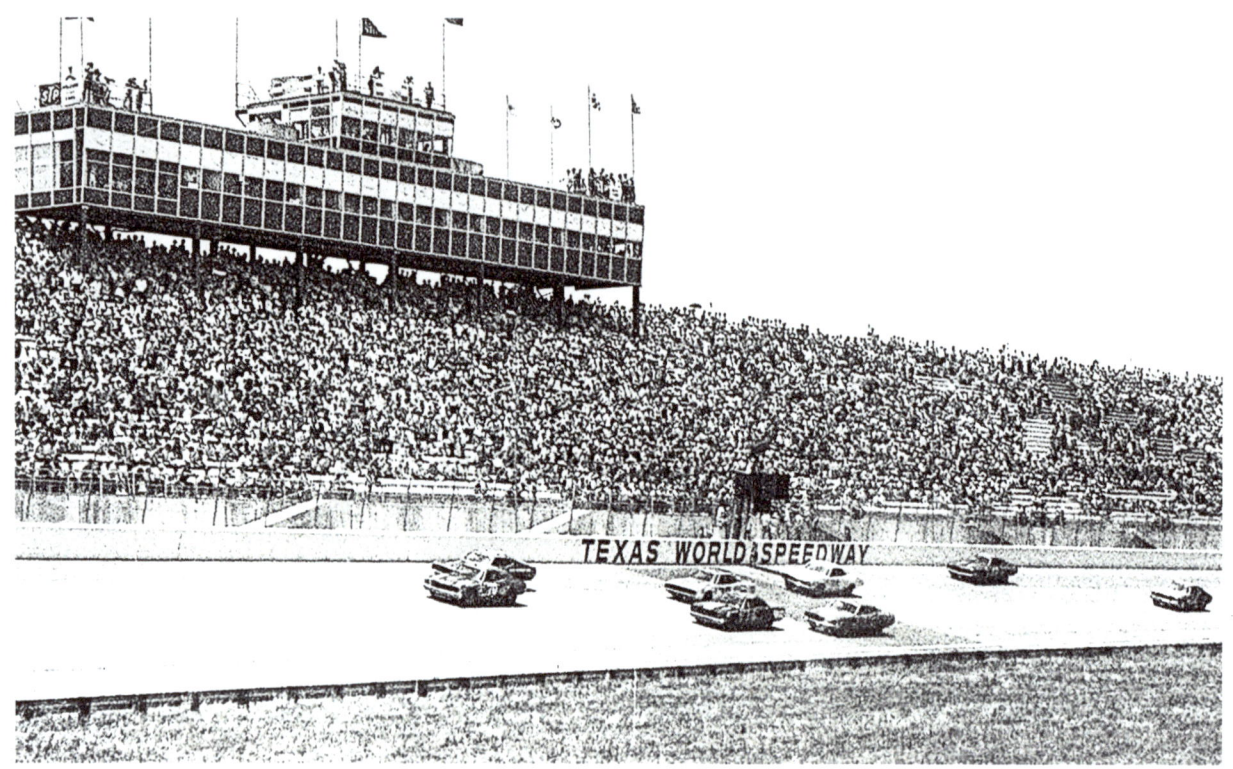

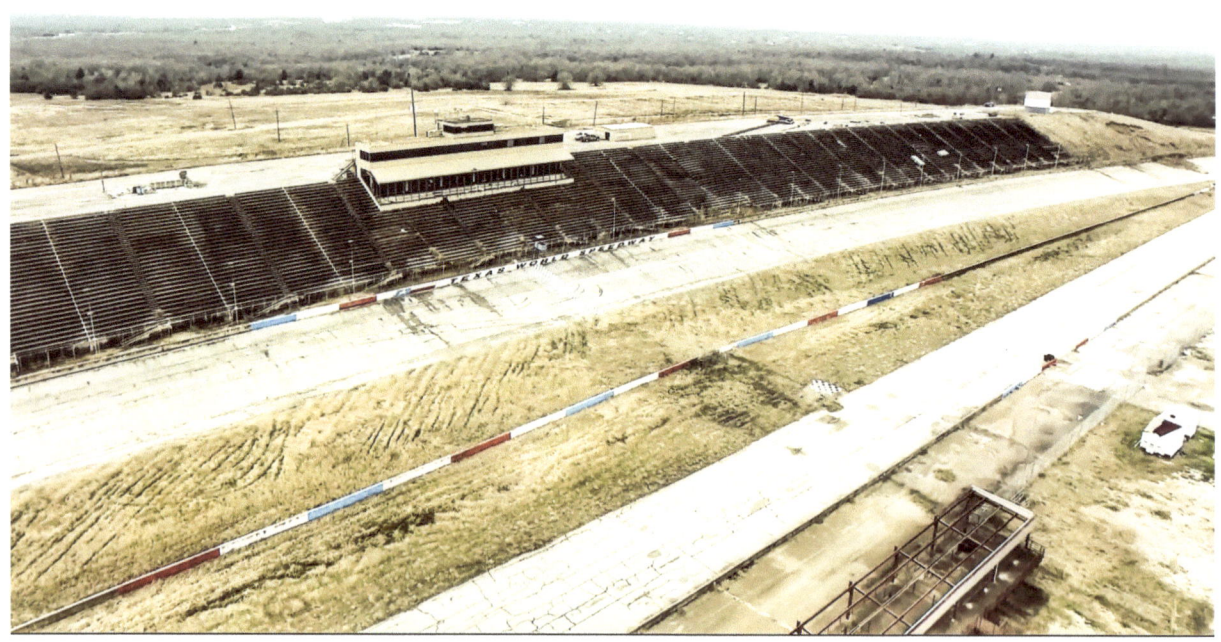